THE HOT SAUCE COOKBOOK

THE HOT SAUCE COOKBOOK

The Book of Fiery Salsa and
Hot Sauce Recipes

ROCKRIDGE
PRESS

ISBN Print 978-1-62315-365-6 | eBook 978-1-62315-366-3

CONTENTS

INTRODUCTION

When it comes to chiles, the joke is on Mother Nature. These bright and attractive fruits were naturally engineered with a defense mechanism meant to cause pain and repel mammals wanting them for a snack. But if their spicy hot flavor is unpleasant and irritating, why have humans sought them out for thousands of years? Because as soon as we feel the hot sting from a chile, our bodies release pain-killing endorphins that are stronger than morphine and just as addictive.

A convenient vehicle for getting that chile rush is via hot sauce. But while there is a wide abundance of hot sauce varieties available at most supermarkets, it wasn't always that way. Few folks cared about chiles until the 1980s, when the popularity of Southwestern cuisine piqued interest in spicy chiles. Then in the 1990s, people discovered an array of hot sauces beyond the ubiquitous Tabasco brand. Producing and eating really hot sauce was still considered just an eccentric fad, but today chile conventions, festivals, and institutes are dedicated to exploring everything about these spicy plants. Farmers, both professional and amateur, hybridize chiles to constantly produce new varieties, some specifically seeking the title of hottest chile in the world.

As noted by Dr. Paul Bosland (popularly known as the "Chileman"), professor of horticulture at New Mexico State University, the number of chile varieties is staggering, and there is an equal amount of information about them yet to be discovered. In Austin, Texas, Dr. Jean Andrews (also known as "The Pepper Lady") also took interest in organizing the world of chiles, and published two books on the subject: *Peppers, the Domesticated Capsicums* in 1984 and *The Pepper Trail: History and Recipes from Around the World* in 1999. Both still remain the definitive sources for chile history and ethnobotany. The first chile-centric periodical, *Chile Pepper* magazine, was founded by Dave DeWitt and published in 1987. Since then, countless books and websites have been published and dedicated solely to chiles and hot sauces.

The public took an interest in chiles in the 1980s, but these plants have a long history in cuisine, dating back seven thousand years. There is a lot of confusion about the difference between chiles and peppers—if there is any difference at all. Chapter one untangles the mystery of chile nomenclature and introduces some of the most popular and recognizable hot sauces made and sold around the world today.

Depending on where you are in the country, most grocery stores carry at least a few chiles or hot sauces with familiar flavors. You can always count on fresh bell peppers, pickled jalapeños, Tabasco sauce, red pepper flakes, and ground cayenne pepper, but there are hundreds more to try. Chapter two explores a small cross-section of chiles and their heat levels, from warm to scorching.

Chapter three covers some basic ingredients, equipment, and cooking methods needed for successful hot sauce. Be sure to carefully read how to properly handle chiles and how to safely store the sauce once it's made. Don't miss the ten tips for how to make great hot sauce.

Chapters four through eight have over seventy-five hot sauce recipes and dishes in which to use them. Start with hot sauces from Central America, the Southwest, and Louisiana, and then move on to blazing hot sauces from the West Indies and the Caribbean. Try out some easy Asian hot sauces, including Thai, Chinese, Korean, Indian, and Turkish recipes. Last, explore hot sauces from Hawaii, South America, Spain, Mozambique, and Tunisia. And then, of course, you can always try out your own flavor combinations.

PART ONE

HOT SAUCE BASICS

CHAPTER ONE

GETTING STARTED

What Is a Hot Sauce, Anyway?

In the United States, there are always a few iconic bottles of hot sauce on grocery store shelves and almost everyone has at least one in his or her refrigerator. In fact, all over the world, different cultures have some kind of hot sauce. Thailand has sriracha. Piri piri can be found in Africa and Portugal. And Jamaica is known for its jerk.

A hot sauce is basically any spicy, pungent condiment that contains some type of chile combined with vinegar, oil, vegetables, fruit, and other spices. But is there a difference between a chile or a pepper or a chili? Depending on what country, state, or region you're in, a chile might be referred to as a chili, chilli, aji, sweet pepper, hot pepper, capsicum, pimentón, paprika, or just pepper. Simply put, there is no difference, and all of these names can be used interchangeably.

The confusion in nomenclature may stem from Columbus's arrival in the West Indies. While in search of exotic foreign spices coveted in Europe, like ginger, cinnamon, and black pepper, he found what the natives referred to as chiles or "xilli," an Aztec Nahuatl word. They were hot and spicy like the familiar black peppercorns, so Columbus called them "pimiento," which means pepper in Spanish. Contrary to Columbus's name, hot chile peppers are not related to black pepper at all. All hot chile peppers, or capsicums, are the fruit of the plants from the genus *Capsicum* (black pepper is from the genus *Piper*). The hot spice that they impart is called capsaicin, which varies from chile to chile. The only chile that has no capsaicin is the bell pepper, hence its mild, nonspicy yet sweet flavor. All chiles are from the same species, but only five of these species are widely domesticated. Within the species are thousands of varieties, and new varieties are constantly being hybridized and cultivated.

Hot Sauces Around the World

Unlike many other vegetables and fruits, hot chiles grow all over the world and consequently are found in many cuisines. Their oldest origin has been traced back seven thousand years, where remnants of chiles were found at prehistoric Peruvian burial grounds. More evidence of chile cultivation was found in Mexican cave dwellings in 3400 B.C.E., and also Southwestern Pueblo tribes in 900 C.E.

Chiles grew wild over all of South America, much of Mexico, and the southern tip of Texas. Birds expanded the sprawl of chiles even more. They are immune to capsicum, so when they ate these chiles, they carried the seeds and dispersed them far and wide. The chiles themselves were very easy to transport, so Columbus was able to return to Spain from the Americas bringing chiles, thereby introducing them to Europe, and Portuguese explorers introduced them to Asia. Today chile sauces belong to every continent on earth and one can find signature hot sauces from cuisines all over the globe.

Each sauce has a few ingredients or methods that are indicative of its style. Some sauces reflect a combination of cultures and cuisines, but among the hundreds of traditional hot sauces, the following are some of the most recognizable. They are easy to find on grocery-store shelves or to make yourself at home.

Louisiana-style hot sauce is known for its blend of red chiles, like tabasco or cayenne peppers, which are combined with vinegar and salt, and can be fermented for years to develop flavor. Brands like Crystal,

Louisiana, Texas Pete's, and Frank's Red Hot are among the most well known in this category. Perhaps the most ubiquitous Louisiana-style hot sauce is Tabasco, first produced in 1868 by Edmund McIlhenny on Avery Island, Louisiana. Today, the Tabasco brand has expanded from their original recipe to produce flavors like chipotle, green jalapeño, Buffalo, and habanero to compete with the expanding hot sauce market.

Called "pepper sauce," hot sauces in the Caribbean islands are extremely spicy and often feature tropical fruits combined with very hot chiles, most notably the Scotch bonnet. This close cousin of the habanero pepper may also be called Bahama Mama, Scotty Bons, or Bonney pepper. This distinctive Caribbean ingredient is fresh, fruity, and one of the hottest chiles on record (see the Scoville scale on page 18 to find out how hot). It is found in jerk seasoning, a common flavoring found throughout the islands. Though usually used as a marinade, many enjoy jerk sauce as a condiment too. "Jerk" is also part of a method of barbecuing that dates back twelve hundred years to the native Arawak Indians, originally from what is today Guyana, and to the Caribs from South America. They used a mixture of chiles, spices, and garlic rubbed onto their meat and then cooked it slowly over a hot wooden grate known as a Barbacoa. Today dry jerk spice blends and jerk sauces are used for chicken, pork, goat, beef, and fish.

Fiery red may be the color most associated with hot sauce, but plenty of green sauces have a good amount of heat too. Many cuisines have their own version of *salsa verde* (which translates to "green sauce"), so the name can be confusing. Italians make it with fresh green herbs like parsley, basil, garlic, anchovies, capers, and olive oil. Argentine green sauce, or chimichurri, has parsley, vinegar, garlic, and oil, and can have a little or a lot of red pepper flakes. There are also nonspicy versions in French and German cuisines. Latin and New Mexican green sauces, on the other hand, are spicier and contain green chiles like jalapeños, serrano, or poblanos. One popular brand, El Yucateco, uses green habaneros and has an assertive kick to it.

One of the most popular Asian hot sauces right now is sriracha, which is named after the coastal city of Si Racha, in Thailand. Most people in the United States are familiar with the Huy Fong recipe made by Chinese-Vietnamese immigrant David Tran, but in Thailand, Thanom Chakkapak concocted the original Sriraja Panich sauce in 1930. She meant it to be used as a spicy cocktail sauce to accompany the seafood diet eaten in the port town, but today the iconic bottle with the rooster and green top can be found on grocery store shelves and restaurant tables everywhere. The sweet, tangy, and spicy blend of red chiles, vinegar, garlic, sugar, and salt adorns anything from American foods like hot dogs and pizza to Asian dishes like chow mein and phở.

In the infinite category of Mexican hot sauces and salsas, you can find hundreds of combinations of a variety of chiles like chipotles, New Mexico red chiles, habaneros, or cascabel, along with earthy ingredients like tomatoes and pumpkin seeds.

There are also non-tomato-based hot sauces in Mexican cuisine. Cholula, a popular brand that is recognizable by its carved wooden cap, is produced just outside of Guadalajara in Mexico. The hundred-year-old recipe is very closely guarded. It is a blend of árbol and piquín chiles, water, vinegar, spices, and salt and has a mildly spicy and tangy, yet balanced, flavor.

Harissa is a less-commercially known hot sauce used mainly in Moroccan, Algerian, and Tunisian cuisine. It may include garlic, olive oil, and aromatic spices such as caraway, coriander, or cumin, and can be mild or fiery depending on what kind of chiles are in the mix. It pairs well with its native North African cuisines as well as Mediterranean dishes. You can find it commercially in tubes, cans, or jars at well-stocked grocery stores or Middle Eastern markets, but spice levels vary wildly. A customized homemade version is easy to make and guarantees the right punch of heat (see page 136).

CHAPTER TWO

GLORIOUS CHILES

Chiles and Their Flavors

Whether fresh, dried, ground, pickled, or canned, each chile has a unique flavor. The variety in shape, thickness, and heat level lend each to different styles of cooking, cuisines, and dishes. Dried chiles will have more intense, concentrated flavors that are good for moles and deeply flavored sauces, while fresh chiles can be roasted, sautéed, grilled, or puréed. Use chopped fresh chiles to add texture to salsa for dipping or to ceviche for heat and crunch.

Flavors can range from vegetal and grassy in some green peppers like jalapeños and shishitos, or fruity and citrusy in Scotch bonnets and aji amarillo. Capsaicin manifests itself differently depending on the pepper. In some peppers the heat will zap your tongue, while the heat in others will latch onto your mouth and lips, lingering there. Other peppers will creep to the back of your throat with an intense, slowly building heat.

The Scoville Scale

To measure this heat, the Scoville organoleptic heat scale was invented in 1912 by pharmacologist Wilbur Scoville. Its purpose was to assign a numeric value to the spice levels of chiles. He devised a calculation of how many parts of sugar water were necessary to dilute a solution of capsaicin oil made from dried chiles until human tasters could no longer detect the heat. This calculation was known as Scoville units. The higher the rating, the more the oil must be diluted, and therefore the hotter the pepper.

Using humans to measure the units was highly subjective, so now a process called high performance liquid chromatography, or HPLC, measures the amount of capsaicinoids (capsaicin) in parts per million. Scoville's original terms are still used for reporting, but the HPLC process is more accurate and is the standard by which spice levels of chiles—as well as of spices and hot sauces—are judged today.

Fresh Chiles

Here are some of the more common fresh chiles available today:

Aji Amarillo is a common Peruvian chile that is about 4 to 6 inches long with thick flesh and full-bodied fruit and citrus notes. Though used often in Peruvian cuisine, it is a bit difficult to find fresh unless at a Peruvian market, where it may also be canned, sold as a paste, or dried.
SU: 30,000–50,000 (Note: SU refers to the Scoville unit.)

Aji Rojo is another common Peruvian chile, but despite its name (*rojo* means red in Spanish) it is more of an orange-red color than true red. It is similar in heat level to a cayenne pepper and is often added raw to ceviche. It is harvested in August through October, though difficult to find fresh in the United States.
SU: 40,000–50,000

Anaheim may also be called the **Long Green Chile** or **California Green Chile**. This easy-to-find pepper is large in shape and mild in heat with a clear, vegetal, slightly sweet flavor and mild pungency. Look for pods about 5 to 6 inches long in summer months for the best flavor. It's good for stuffing, but remove the tough outer skins when possible.

SU: 1000–1500

Bell Peppers are the most well-known chile, with a mild, juicy flesh. Capsaicin-free, they seem like a chile outlier. Almost every grocery store carries one variety of bell pepper, and depending on their ripeness or color (green, yellow, orange, red, brown, or purple), flavors range from vegetal to sweet.

SU: 0–10

Cayenne, also called **Finger Chile**, is about 2 to 6 inches long. Originally from Mexico, they were brought to Avery Island, Louisiana, to be used in the production of Tabasco hot sauce. Green cayennes appear in summer, but hotter, bright-red cayennes ripen in fall. Dried powder is available everywhere, and the fresh chile is fairly easy to find.

SU: 30,000–50,000

Chiltepin peppers are small (less than a half-inch), spicy, and also referred to as **Bird Pepper** or **Flea Pepper** (the word *tepin* is derived from the Nuhuatl word meaning "flea"). This pre-Columbian chile grows wild in the Southwest and Mexico.

SU: 50,000–100,000

Fresno chiles are similar to jalapeños, but have thinner walls. Look for less-spicy green Fresnos in the summer and hotter ripe ones in the fall in most well-stocked grocery stores.

SU: 2500–10,000

Ghost Chile, also called **Naga Viper** or **Bhut Jolokia**, is a small 2- to 3-inch pepper with a formidable flavor and a heat profile that starts out sweet for the first 45 seconds; its piercing heat sets in and continues to intensify over 10 to 15 minutes. After 30 minutes, the intensity will just begin to subside, but keep in mind that it is one of the hottest chiles on record today and can be dangerous if not handled properly. (See page 26 for more on proper handling.)

SU: 1, 350,000

Habanero chiles are thought to be from Mexico, but since they have no Mayan name, and *habanero* actually means "from Havana," these peppers could be Caribbean. These easier-to-find cousins to the Caribbean Scotch bonnet chile are very hot, have a fruity perfume, and are best in summer months when they ripen to yellow or red. Green or brown habaneros can also be found, but orange is the most common.

SU: 100,000–350,000

Hot Cherry, Cherry Peppers, or Creole Cherry Peppers vary in size and shape, but are usually about 1 to 2 inches long and round or triangular in shape. These easy-to-find peppers are good for pickling alone or with other vegetables.

SU: 2500–5000

Jalapeños are very common chiles found in most grocery stores. They have thick, juicy walls; are about 2 to 3 inches long; and most often are green in color. They have a vegetal flavor and though available year-round, have the best flavor in late summer.

SU: 2500–5000

Malagueta chiles are not to be confused with the unrelated West African spice of a similar name, which is more akin to cardamom or ginger. These peppers are a staple in Brazilian, Portuguese, and African (Mozambique) cooking and may also be called **Piri Piri Peppers**. When mature, they turn from green to red and are about 2 inches long, but they may also be larger.

SU: 50,000–100,000

New Mexico Green Chiles are large in size and similar to Anaheim chiles. They peak in late summer and have a sweet, earthy flavor. They're widely available and easy to find at well-stocked grocery stores.

SU: 100–1000

Padrón Peppers are Spanish chiles from Galicia in northern Spain. They're usually harvested young, when their green flesh is tender and the seeds are not yet mature. They have a mild nutty flavor. June- and July- harvested peppers are less spicy than those harvested in August and September, but occasionally a spicy pepper will sneak into a mild bunch. Though not yet widely available, these peppers are gaining popularity and can be found in well-stocked grocery stores.

SU: 1000–2500

Piquín Peppers, also spelled **Pequín**, have a complex, nutty citrus flavor. They grow wild throughout Mexico, but can also be found dried in Mexican markets.

SU: 50,000–100,000

Poblano Chiles are heart-shaped with thick, dark, green fleshy walls. These easy-to-find peppers are best in summer months and are ideal for chiles rellenos.

SU: 2500–5000

Scotch Bonnets are closely related to habaneros and often used interchangeably. Though found mainly in the Caribbean, their popularity is growing so they're easier to find. They vary in color from green to red and have a fresh and fruity flavor coupled with a strong heat factor.

SU: 100,000–325,000

Serrano chiles have thick, juicy walls and are usually found in their less-ripe green state, though their ripe red counterpart is similar in spice level. They have a clear vegetal flavor and are about $1\frac{1}{2}$ to $2\frac{1}{2}$ inches long.

SU: 6000–15,000

Shishito Peppers are bright, glossy green, curvy, and wrinkled, with grassy and citrus flavors. Unless in season, which peaks from May through September, they can be hard to find. These mild Japanese peppers are usually eaten panfried or grilled and seasoned with salt.

SU: 50–200

Tabasco chiles have distinct piercing heat with an herbal flavor and are well known for the hot sauce with the same name. These 2-inch-long peppers are usually harvested while green and allowed to mature to a much spicier red color. Look for them in well-stocked grocery stores.

SU: 30,000–100,000

Thai Chiles, also called **Thai Bird Peppers**, are usually seen in Southeast Asian cuisine and come in either green or red. They have an intense lingering heat and are good to add to dishes where you want spice but not a lot of chiles.

SU: 50,000–100,000

Dried Chiles

Here are some of the more common dried chiles available today:

Ancho chiles are dried, ripe poblanos that are brownish black in color and wrinkled, with a sweet, mild, rich flavor. They're commonly used in Mexican cuisine and are easy to find.

SU: 1000–1500

Chiles de Árbol are small, thin, and long with a decent kick of heat. They can also be found fresh by the same name, but are more easily available dried.

SU: 15,000–30,000

California chiles are dried Anaheims that are mild in flavor. They are very easy to find.

SU: 500–2500

Cascabel chiles, also called **Rattle Chiles**, get their name from the sound the loose seeds make when shaken. They have a tannic and slightly smoky flavor.

SU: 1500–2500

Chipotles are smoked jalapeños that are often canned with adobo sauce. They are spicy yet smoky and sweet in flavor.

SU: 2500–5000

Guajillo chiles have a thin, deep red flesh that's smooth and shiny with a flavor like green tea with berry undertones. They are common in most well-stocked grocery stores and Mexican markets.

SU: 2500–5000

Guntur Sannam, from India, is a bright red chile with lots of seeds. It is harvested from December to May, but is most often finely chopped and dried into flakes. These red chile flakes or red pepper flakes are commonly sprinkled on pizza and pasta.

SU: 30,500–40,000

Pasilla peppers are dried chilaca chiles. They are black and wrinkled, and about 7 to 9 inches long. Their concentrated raisin flavor is often found in Mexican moles. When shopping for pasillas, beware that they are sometimes mislabeled as anchos.

SU: 1000–1500

SCOVILLE SCALE	UNITS OF HEAT
FRESH CHILES	
Trinidad Moruga Scorpion	2,009,231
Ghost Chile (a.k.a. Naga Viper, Bhut Jolokia)	1,350,000
Adjuma	100,000–500,000
Habanero	100,000–350,000
Scotch Bonnet	100,000–325,000
Rocoto	50,000–250,000
Thai Chile	50,000–100,000
Chiltepin	50,000–100,000
Malagueta	50,000–100,000
Piquín (Pequín)	50,000–100,000
Aji Rojo	40,000–50,000
Tabasco	30,000–100,000
Aji Amarillo	30,000–50,000
Cayenne	30,000–50,000
Serrano	6000–15,000
Peter Pepper	5000–30,000
Cascabel	2500–8000
Hungarian Wax	2500–8000
Hot Cherry	2500–5000
Fresno	2500–10,000
Poblano	2500–5000
Jalapeño	2500–5000
Padrón	1000–2500
Anaheim	1000–1500
New Mexico Green Chile	100–1000
Pepperoncini	100–500
Cubanelle	50–1000
Shishito	50–200
Banana Pepper	0–500
Bell Pepper	0–10

SCOVILLE SCALE	UNITS OF HEAT
DRIED CHILES	
Guntur Sannam	30,500–40,000
Chile de Árbol	15,000–30,000
New Mexico Red Chile	3500–8000
Chipotles	2500–5000
Guajillo	2500–5000
Mirasol	2500–5000
Cascabel	1500–2500
Ancho	1000–1500
Mulatto	1000–1500
Pasilla	1000–1500
California	500–2500

CHAPTER THREE

COOKING WITH FIRE

Ingredients

Hot sauce is packed with flavor and together with chiles, there are a few other ingredients that complement the heat to create a sauce. Most of the ingredients are easily available at your local grocery store, but also be sure to investigate ethnic grocery stores or buy supplies online.

Low-Sodium Chicken Broth

Commercial brands of chicken broth are filled with sodium that can make your hot sauce unexpectedly salty. Make sure to buy products only marked as "low sodium" or use homemade chicken stock.

Chayote

This is a gourd common to Caribbean cuisine, similar in texture to zucchini or summer squash. It goes by many aliases, like chocho, mirliton, christophene, or vegetable pear. Females have smooth skin, while males have prickly skin; the female fruit is easier to find and prepare. Look for chayotes that are firm and free from blemishes. Discard the tough pit.

Fish Sauce

This is an Asian condiment made from fermented anchovies and salt that is most often used in Thai, Vietnamese, and Filipino cuisines. It has a very pungent odor and adds deep umami flavor to food, akin to the effects of Worcestershire sauce.

Garlic Powder

This is dried garlic ground into a fine powder. Garlic granules are also dried garlic, but in a coarser grind. Do not confuse garlic salt, which is a mixture of garlic and salt, for garlic powder.

Kochujang, Gochujang, or Korean Chili Paste

This is a savory paste made from fermented soybeans, glutinous rice, red chiles, and salt. It can be found in jars or small plastic tubs in Korean markets.

Kochukaru, Gochugaru, or Korean Red Pepper

This is made from dried red chiles and is what gives kimchi its spice. Find it in Korean markets in large resealable plastic bags, in different grades of coarseness and spiciness. Choose a grade based on your personal preference.

Freshly Squeezed Lemon, Lime, or Orange Juice

Be sure to always use citrus juice that's freshly squeezed. Shelf-stable juices usually have additives or have been pasteurized, muddying their bright, fresh flavor.

Mae Ploy

This is a sweet chili sauce that's usually found in the Asian section of supermarkets.

Mexican Oregano

This relative of lemon verbena has a milder taste than the more familiar Mediterranean varieties. It can be found in Latin markets or in the Latin section of supermarkets. You may substitute any other variety.

Mirin

This is a sweet Japanese cooking wine with low alcohol content. Look for it in the Asian section of the supermarket.

Fine Salt

This should be used for all of the recipes in this book unless otherwise noted. Look for a pure and uniodized salt, such as fine sea salt. Since the grains of kosher salt are coarser, keep in mind that if you use it as a substitute, more might be needed.

Fine Kosher Salt

Make sure to use a product specifically marked as "fine" or the salt ratios in the final dish will be off.

Coarse White Hawaiian Salt

This pure and untreated salt is evaporated using only the sun.

Tomato Purée

This is purely flash-cooked puréed tomatoes. Do not confuse it with tomato sauce that could have added ingredients, which can add odd flavors to your hot sauce.

Tomatillos

These fruits are greenish yellow in color, average 2 inches in diameter, and are encased in papery husks that need to be removed. Their tart flavor has hints of lemon, sour apple, and herbs. Although tomatillos can ripen to yellow, they are generally used while still green and quite firm.

Vinegar

Many kinds of vinegar are used for hot sauces depending on the desired flavor of the hot sauce:

Distilled white vinegar is a no-frills, inexpensive, and colorless vinegar with a bracing acidity, often used in Caribbean hot sauces as a preservative.

Cider vinegar, often seen in Southwestern cuisine, has a distinct fruity flavor imparted by the apple pulp that it's made from. It has strong acidity and is a cloudy brown color.

Sherry vinegar is made from fermenting the sherry wines of Jerez, Spain. This vinegar is dark in color with a more complex, less sharp flavor.

Purified Water

Water that has been purified to remove any contaminants or chemicals that can impart odd flavors to pickled, preserved, or fermented hot sauces.

Cooking Equipment and Methods

A few pieces of equipment and a couple of methods are used repeatedly to make most of the hot-sauce recipes featured in this book. Have the equipment ready to go before you begin to make the process easier and faster.

Nonreactive Cookware

Stainless steel pots or pans are a necessity when cooking salty or acidic food like hot sauce, in order to avoid metallic flavors and off colors. Do not use cast iron, copper, or aluminum cookware.

Glass Jars

Jars that are sterilized should be used to store your hot sauces. Sterilization removes bacteria, yeast, or fungi that can lead to contamination and early spoilage of food.

Food Processor and Blender

Both are necessary to get smooth hot sauces with the right texture. The food processor will do the best job chopping drier mixtures and will leave sauces with a bit more texture. Use a blender for sauces with more moisture to get a very smooth sauce.

Kitchen Scale

This is useful for recipes where weights are given to get accurate measurements for produce that is non-uniform in size.

Spice Grinder

Use this to pulverize and grind spices quickly and uniformly. This tool is indispensable for those who often use toasted whole spices. If you don't have one, substitute a mortar and pestle or a spare coffee grinder.

Rubber Spatulas

These are best for scraping sauces out of food processors and blenders. Use silicone spatulas when cooking, as they can withstand high heat.

Mesh Strainers

These are a necessity for smooth hot sauces. It's best to have one fine mesh and one medium mesh strainer, depending on how thoroughly you want to strain your sauce.

Large Measuring Cup

One with a spout is helpful when transferring hot sauces to jars or bottles. A funnel works well, too.

Toasting Chiles or Spices

This should be done in a hot, dry pan. Shake the pan often until the chiles or spices are aromatic. It should take only a few minutes.

Rehydrate Dried Chiles

Rehydrate any dried chiles in hot or warm water until pliable but not mushy. Never boil dried chiles, as it destroys their flavors.

Charring

Charring ingredients like chiles, tomatoes, and garlic is a simple way to add fire-roasted flavor to your hot sauce. It can be easily done under a broiler in a few minutes. If you have gas burners, you can char chiles directly over the flame, turning them with tongs as the skin begins to blacken.

Safety and Storage

Chiles and hot sauces are delicious, but improper handling or storage can be dangerous. Follow a few general guidelines before you begin. When working with chiles, know if you have a very spicy or less spicy variety of chile or how much capsaicin it contains. Hotter chiles require more care to keep the capsaicin contained.

For safe chile handling, wear powder-free latex gloves, food handler's gloves, or plastic wrap as a barrier when preparing and touching the chiles. Always wash your hands thoroughly before touching your eyes, nose, lips, or other sensitive areas on your body. Clean your knives and cutting board immediately after using. Consider wearing goggles to protect your eyes from the fumes. If you touch a chile and your skin starts to tingle and burn, wash with mechanics soap containing pumice. It will remove the capsaicin from your pores. Also remember that capsaicin is alcohol soluble, so rubbing alcohol, as well as gin, vodka, or any other high-proof spirit, can help remove the capsaicin.

Before preparing the recipes in this book, properly ventilate your kitchen. Once capsaicin and vinegar are exposed to heat, their fumes are released into the air and can irritate your nose and eyes, as well as affect breathing. Open windows and turn on fans to disperse the fumes.

When using a blender to blend sauces that are hot from cooking, always remove the small cap from the blender lid and place a kitchen towel over the hole. This will allow the steam to escape from the blender so the lid won't blow off.

To store your finished hot sauce, always use sterilized jars or bottles to avoid contamination. Remember that store-bought sauces have additives to extend their shelf life, but your homemade sauces do not, so refrigerate them and adhere to the suggested expiration dates in the recipes.

If you happen to overindulge or a hot sauce is spicier than expected, quell the heat in your mouth by ingesting dairy such as milk, ice cream, or yogurt. Stay away from anything carbonated like beer or soda; even though they are refreshing, the tiny bubbles give the sensation of intensifying the heat.

Ten Tips for Making Great Hot Sauce

1. The spiciness of a chile can be estimated, but never guaranteed, so a good rule of thumb is that the smaller in size, the hotter the chile. However, remember that spice levels, even between two chiles grown on the same plant, can differ. That is why the Scoville scale offers a range.
2. If you're working with a variety of chiles for the first time and are worried about a too-spicy sauce, remove the seeds and the white membranes from the interior to reduce the heat.
3. When buying fresh chiles, look for ones that seem heavy for their size, with tight, shiny skin free of blemishes. To help them retain

their moisture, wrap them in paper towels (not in plastic bags), and refrigerate.

4. When buying dried chiles, look for softness and suppleness. Avoid dusty, cracked, or faded chiles. Store them in an airtight container in a cool, dark spot.

5. If you do have dried chiles that have become brittle, put them in an airtight bag with a piece of paper towel that is just damp, and seal the bag. Let them sit overnight and the next day your chiles will be supple again.

6. Vegetables vary in size, so stick to weight measurements when possible. If numerals are given, choose medium-sized produce for more accurate results.

7. Remember that chlorinated water kills fermentation, so use purified water when called for in a recipe.

8. Make sure you have all of your ingredients and equipment ready, and read through the entire recipe before beginning. You don't want to be surprised by a 2-week fermentation time or be caught without storage containers!

9. Know that you can always add to the recipes but you can't take away, so taste your sauces as you go and when you've finished preparing them. Add extra seasoning to suit your taste and make notes for next time.

10. Get creative! These recipes are just the beginning. Mix your hot sauces with other condiments like mayo, honey, mustard, ketchup, barbecue sauce, and salsa to make even more simple and easy spicy sauces. Stir them into soups, stews, or softened butter to add spice whenever and wherever you desire.

PART TWO

RECIPES

CHAPTER FOUR

CENTRAL AMERICA AND THE SOUTHWEST

Pace-Style Picante Sauce

YIELD: ABOUT 3½ CUPS

This chunky, tomato-based sauce simmers for about half an hour to let the flavors meld. Scoop it up with tortilla chips or spoon it onto scrambled eggs.

2 CUPS CANNED TOMATO PURÉE

1½ CUPS WATER

½ CUP CHOPPED WHITE ONION

2 JALAPEÑO CHILES, FINELY CHOPPED

¼ CUP DISTILLED WHITE VINEGAR

¼ TEASPOON GARLIC POWDER

½ TEASPOON FINE SALT

1. In a large saucepan over medium heat, combine all of the ingredients and bring to a boil. Reduce the heat to medium low and let simmer, stirring occasionally, for 30 to 45 minutes, or until thickened. Season with salt, if necessary.

2. Remove the saucepan from the heat, and let the sauce cool to room temperature. Transfer to an airtight container and refrigerate for up to 1 week.

New Mexican Roasted Green Chile Sauce

YIELD: ABOUT 3 CUPS

Stir roasted chicken, white kidney beans, and fresh corn into this green sauce for an easy chicken stew.

3 ANAHEIM CHILES, STEMMED, HALVED LENGTHWISE, AND SEEDED

2 TABLESPOONS VEGETABLE OIL

⅔ CUP CHOPPED WHITE ONION

2 GARLIC CLOVES, FINELY CHOPPED

2 TABLESPOONS ALL-PURPOSE FLOUR

1½ CUPS LOW-SODIUM CHICKEN BROTH

½ TEASPOON FINE SALT

1. Preheat the broiler and arrange a rack in the middle of the oven. Put the chiles on a baking sheet, cut-side down. Drizzle with 1 tablespoon of the oil. Broil until blackened and charred, about 15 minutes, rotating the pan as necessary. Transfer the chiles to a cutting board and cut into a ¼-inch dice; set aside.

2. In a medium saucepan over medium heat, heat the remaining 1 table-spoon oil. Add the onion and garlic, and cook, stirring occasionally, until the onion is softened, about 5 minutes. Sprinkle in the flour, stir to coat the vegetables, and cook 1 to 2 minutes. Add the broth, salt, and the reserved chiles and stir to combine. Increase the heat to high and bring to a boil. Let cook until thickened, an additional 5 to 10 minutes. Season with salt, if necessary. Use immediately or let cool and transfer to an airtight container and refrigerate for up to 1 week.

New Mexican Red Sauce

YIELD: ABOUT 2½ CUPS

Make this sauce in a large quantity and freeze smaller portions in containers after step three. Defrost and add the final ingredients in step four when you'd like freshly made sauce.

12 DRIED NEW MEXICO RED OR CALIFORNIA CHILES,
 RINSED AND STEMMED
2 CUPS WATER
1 TEASPOON FINE SALT
2 TABLESPOONS VEGETABLE OIL
1 TABLESPOON ALL-PURPOSE FLOUR
½ TEASPOON DRIED OREGANO
½ TEASPOON GARLIC POWDER
½ TEASPOON GROUND CUMIN

1. In a large saucepan over high heat, combine the chiles and water, and bring to a simmer. Reduce the heat to low and let simmer until the chiles are plump and soft, about 10 minutes.

2. Taste the chile water, and if bitter, drain the chiles and add 2 cups of fresh water. If not bitter, transfer the cooking water and chiles to a blender. Add the salt. Remove the small cap in the blender lid, place the lid on the blender, and cover the hole with a kitchen towel. Blend until smooth, stopping to scrape down the sides with a rubber spatula as necessary.

3. Place a mesh strainer over a medium bowl. Pour the sauce into the strainer and stir with a rubber spatula. Discard the solids in the strainer.

4. In a large frying pan over high heat, heat the oil. Add the flour and stir with a wooden spoon until smooth. Add the chile purée, oregano, garlic powder, and cumin, and stir to combine. Let cook until thickened, about 10 minutes. Season with salt, if necessary. Use immediately or let cool and transfer to an airtight container. Refrigerate for up to 1 week.

Citrus Chipotle Salsa

MAKES 2 CUPS

A smoky and sweet sauce to complement roasted pork tenderloin medallions or a steak-filled burrito.

10 DRIED GUAJILLO CHILES, STEMMED AND SEEDED

1 CUP WATER, PLUS MORE FOR SOAKING THE CHILES

3 TABLESPOONS FRESHLY SQUEEZED LEMON JUICE

3 TABLESPOONS FRESHLY SQUEEZED LIME JUICE

3 CHIPOTLE CHILES IN ADOBO SAUCE

1 TEASPOON VEGETABLE OIL

¾ TEASPOON FINE SALT

½ TEASPOON ONION POWDER

1. Place the guajillo chiles in a large bowl, add enough water to cover them, and let sit until softened, about 30 minutes.

2. Drain the chiles and transfer to a blender. Add the remaining 1 cup of water and the remaining ingredients. Blend until smooth, stopping and scraping down the sides of the blender with a rubber spatula if necessary, about 1 to 2 minutes. Transfer to an airtight container and refrigerate for up to 2 weeks.

Roasted Tomato Salsa

A quick trip under the broiler gives the vegetables in this smooth tomato salsa charred flavor. Use it as a dip for chips or as a topping on cheesy quesadillas.

1 POBLANO CHILE, STEMMED AND HALVED LENGTHWISE

1 POUND RIPE TOMATOES, CORED AND HALVED

½ MEDIUM WHITE ONION, CUT INTO ½-INCH SLICES

2 GARLIC CLOVES, PEELED AND SMASHED

1 JALAPEÑO CHILE, STEMMED

½ TEASPOON FINE SALT

2 TABLESPOONS COARSELY CHOPPED FRESH CILANTRO

1 TEASPOON FRESHLY SQUEEZED LIME JUICE

1. Preheat the broiler to high and arrange a rack on the upper level.

2. Put the poblano skin-side up on a baking sheet and broil until it just starts to release some juices, about 5 minutes. Put the tomato halves skin-side up on the baking sheet with the poblano, and scatter the onion, garlic, and jalapeño onto the sheet. Broil until the poblano and tomato skins start to blacken and blister, about 7 minutes more.

3. Transfer everything to a blender, add the salt, and blend until smooth. Transfer to a medium heatproof bowl and let cool to room temperature.

4. Stir in the cilantro and lime juice. Season with more salt and lime juice if needed. Transfer to an airtight container and refrigerate for up to 1 week.

Smooth Salsa Verde

MAKES ABOUT 2 CUPS

Tart tomatillos paired with fresh cilantro and green chiles make a natural topping for fresh fish tacos.

1 POUND TOMATILLOS, PAPERY SKINS REMOVED
2 SERRANO CHILES, STEMMED AND COARSELY CHOPPED
2 JALAPEÑO CHILES, STEMMED AND COARSELY CHOPPED
2 GARLIC CLOVES, COARSELY CHOPPED
½ CUP COARSELY CHOPPED FRESH CILANTRO
½ TEASPOON FINE SALT

1. Put the tomatillos in a medium saucepan, cover with cold water, and bring to a simmer over medium heat. Cook until the tomatillos are tender but are not falling apart, about 10 minutes.

2. Drain the tomatillos well and place in a blender. Add the remaining ingredients and blend until almost smooth. If necessary, stop occasionally to smash down the tomatillos with a rubber spatula to get the blender blades moving. Do not over blend or the salsa will be thin and watery. Transfer to an airtight container and chill in the refrigerator for at least 1 hour before serving. Refrigerate for up to 4 days.

Mission-Style Roasted Tomato Salsa

MAKES ABOUT 3 CUPS

Toasted pumpkin seeds add a slight creamy texture and árbol chiles add heat to this complex tomato salsa.

1 POUND RIPE TOMATOES, CORED AND HALVED

10 DRIED CHILES DE ÁRBOL, STEMMED AND SEEDED

2 TEASPOONS ANCHO CHILI POWDER

1 TEASPOON FINE SALT

½ TEASPOON GRANULATED SUGAR

1½ CUPS WATER

3 TABLESPOONS UNSALTED HULLED PUMPKIN SEEDS (PEPITAS)

3 TABLESPOONS DISTILLED WHITE VINEGAR

¼ CUP FINELY CHOPPED GREEN ONION (WHITE AND LIGHT GREEN PARTS)

⅓ CUP COARSELY CHOPPED CILANTRO

1. Preheat the broiler to high and arrange a rack in the middle. Line a baking sheet with foil. Put the tomatoes skin-side up on the lined baking sheet and broil until the skins are slightly charred. Transfer to a large saucepan and place over high heat. Add the chiles de árbol, ancho chili powder, salt, sugar, and water. Stir to combine and bring to a boil. Reduce the heat to low, and simmer, stirring often, until the mixture has reduced slightly and thickened, about 20 minutes.

continued ▶

2. Meanwhile, preheat the oven to 350°F. Remove the foil from the baking sheet. Place the pumpkin seeds on the baking sheet and toast until just browned, about 7 to 10 minutes. Remove from the oven and set aside.

3. When the tomato mixture is ready, add the vinegar and cook for 1 minute. Place the mixture in a blender and add the toasted pumpkin seeds. Remove the small cap in the blender lid, place the lid on the blender, and cover the hole with a kitchen towel. Blend until smooth, stopping and scraping the blender with a rubber spatula if necessary.

4. Pour the salsa into a serving bowl and stir in the green onion and cilantro. Refrigerate until chilled before serving, about 3 hours, or transfer to an airtight container and refrigerate for up to 4 days.

Smooth Ancho Chile Salsa

MAKES ABOUT 2½ CUPS

Dried chiles add depth while tomatoes and tomatillos add an acidic kick to this salsa. Mexican oregano adds a mild herbal flavor.

1 TABLESPOON VEGETABLE OIL

½ CUP CHOPPED WHITE ONION

2 GARLIC CLOVES, CHOPPED

2 DRIED ANCHO CHILES, STEMMED, SEEDED,
    AND COARSELY CHOPPED

3 DRIED GUAJILLO CHILES, STEMMED, SEEDED,
    AND COARSELY CHOPPED

8 OUNCES TOMATOES, CORED AND ROUGHLY CHOPPED

8 OUNCES TOMATILLOS, PAPERY HUSKS REMOVED,
    AND ROUGHLY CHOPPED

2 CUPS WATER

1 TABLESPOON DRIED MEXICAN OREGANO

¾ TEASPOON FINE SALT

¼ TEASPOON FRESHLY GROUND PEPPER

½ CUP COARSELY CHOPPED CILANTRO

1. In a medium frying pan over medium heat, heat the oil. Add the onion, garlic, and both dried chiles. Cook, stirring often, for about 5 minutes, or until the onions are soft and the chiles are fragrant.

2. Add the tomatoes and tomatillos, reduce the heat to medium-low, and cook, stirring often, for 10 minutes, or until the tomatoes and tomatillos are just starting to break down.

continued ▶

3. Increase the heat to high, add the water, oregano, salt, and pepper. Bring to a simmer, and reduce the heat to medium-low. Cook for 20 minutes, until slightly thickened.

4. Place the mixture in a blender. Remove the small cap in the blender lid, place the lid on the blender, and cover the hole with a kitchen towel. Blend until smooth, stopping and scraping down the sides of the blender with a rubber spatula if necessary. Pour the salsa into a serving bowl and stir in the cilantro. Refrigerate until chilled before serving, about 3 hours, or transfer to an airtight container and refrigerate for up to 4 days.

Pastor Salsa

Like the classic al pastor *pork tacos marinated with pineapple, this hot sauce uses pineapple for a fresh citrus flavor that's complemented by toasted cumin and cloves.*

1 TEASPOON WHOLE CUMIN SEEDS

2 WHOLE CLOVES

½ TEASPOON DRIED MEXICAN OREGANO

5 DRIED GUAJILLO CHILES, STEMMED AND SEEDED

5 DRIED PASILLA CHILES, STEMMED AND SEEDED

2 DRIED ANCHO CHILES

1 CUP CHOPPED FRESH PINEAPPLE

1 CUP CHOPPED WHITE ONION

2 GARLIC CLOVES, CHOPPED

2 TABLESPOONS CIDER VINEGAR

2 TABLESPOONS FRESHLY SQUEEZED LIME JUICE

¾ TEASPOON FINE SALT

1. In a dry medium frying pan over medium heat, toast the cumin seeds, shaking the pan often, until fragrant, about 2 to 3 minutes. Transfer to a spice grinder and let cool slightly. Add the cloves and oregano to the spice grinder and grind into to a fine powder; set aside.

2. Using the same pan, add the chiles and toast over medium heat, turning occasionally, until fragrant, about 3 to 5 minutes. Transfer the chiles to a medium saucepan, cover with water, and bring to a simmer over high heat. Reduce the heat to medium-low and simmer until soft-ened, about 5 minutes. Remove from the heat.

continued ▶

Pastor Salsa *continued* ▶

3. Taste the chile cooking water, and if not bitter, remove ½ cup. If bitter, measure out ½ cup of fresh water. In a blender, combine the water, chiles, reserved ground spice mix, pineapple, onion, garlic, cider vinegar, lime juice, and salt, and blend on high to a smooth purée. Refrigerate until chilled before serving, about 3 hours, or transfer to an airtight container and refrigerate for up to 4 days.

Salvadoran Salsa Roja

This red sauce is a staple for Salvadoran cuisine. Spoon it over traditional Salvadoran papusas or tamales.

3 TABLESPOONS VEGETABLE OIL

⅓ CUP CHOPPED YELLOW ONION

2 GARLIC CLOVES

1 SERRANO CHILE, FINELY CHOPPED

3 CUPS CHOPPED RIPE TOMATOES

1 TEASPOON DRIED OREGANO

½ TEASPOON FINE SALT

¼ CUP CHOPPED CILANTRO

1. In a large frying pan over medium heat, heat the oil. Add the onion, garlic, and chile. Cook for about 5 minutes, or until the onion is softened.

2. Add the tomatoes, oregano, and salt and stir to combine. Bring to a simmer. Let cook for about 10 minutes, or until the tomatoes begin to break down.

3. Place the mixture in a blender, remove the small cap in the blender lid, place the lid on the blender, and cover the hole with a kitchen towel. Blend until smooth, stopping and scraping the blender with a rubber spatula if necessary. Pour the salsa into a serving bowl and stir in the cilantro. Season with salt, if necessary. Refrigerate until chilled before serving, about 3 hours, or transfer to an airtight container and refrigerate for up to 4 days.

Linzano-Style Costa Rican Salsa

MAKES ABOUT 2 CUPS

Most Costa Rican restaurants have a bottle of Linzano hot sauce on the table ready to be poured over any dish. Its savory deep flavor is like a Costa Rican steak sauce.

1 DRIED GUAJILLO CHILE, STEMMED AND SEEDED

1 DRIED PASILLA CHILE, STEMMED AND SEEDED

1¼ CUPS WATER

½ CUP CHOPPED YELLOW ONION

⅓ CUP CHOPPED CARROT

1 TEASPOON YELLOW MUSTARD SEEDS

1 LOW-SODIUM VEGETABLE BOUILLON CUBE
    OR 1 TEASPOON VEGETABLE BOUILLON GRANULES

2 TABLESPOONS LIGHT BROWN SUGAR

2 TABLESPOONS FRESHLY SQUEEZED LEMON JUICE

1 TABLESPOON DISTILLED WHITE VINEGAR

2 TEASPOONS GROUND CUMIN

2 TEASPOONS FINE SALT

2 TEASPOONS DARK MOLASSES

1. Heat a medium frying pan over medium heat. Tear the chiles into large pieces and add to the pan. Toast, turning occasionally, until fragrant, about 5 minutes. Add the water, onion, carrot, mustard seeds, and bouillon, and reduce the heat to low. Bring to a simmer and let cook, stirring occasionally, until the chiles are softened and the bouillon has dissolved, about 5 minutes.

2. Transfer the mixture to a blender. Add the sugar, lemon juice, vinegar, cumin, salt, and molasses. Remove the small cap in the blender lid, place the lid on the blender, and cover the hole with a kitchen towel. Blend until smooth, stopping and scraping scraping down the sides of the blender with a rubber spatula if necessary. Season with salt if necessary. Transfer to an airtight container and refrigerate until chilled before serving, about 3 hours. Refrigerate for up to 1 week.

Belizean Carrot-Orange Hot Sauce

YIELD: ABOUT 2 CUPS

With eight habaneros, this bright and fruity hot sauce packs a serious punch. The carrots are slightly earthy and sweet to balance the sour citrus juice and cider vinegar.

1 CUP CARROTS, CUT INTO 1-INCH PIECES

8 HABANERO CHILES, SEEDED AND STEMMED

1 NAVEL ORANGE, PEELED AND SEEDS REMOVED

¼ CUP CIDER VINEGAR

3 TABLESPOONS FRESHLY SQUEEZED LIME JUICE

2 TABLESPOONS OLIVE OIL

2 TEASPOONS GRANULATED SUGAR

½ TEASPOON FINE SALT

In a blender, place all of the ingredients and blend until smooth, stopping to scrape down the blender with a rubber spatula if necessary. Transfer to an airtight container and refrigerate for up to 2 weeks.

Black Bean and Green Chile Breakfast Burrito

To add a pop of fresh flavor to your burrito, chop up some tomatoes or avocado to sprinkle over the eggs; then wrap them up in foil and take them to go.

FOR THE REFRIED BEANS:

3 TABLESPOONS VEGETABLE OIL OR LARD

½ CUP FINELY CHOPPED WHITE ONION

2 MEDIUM GARLIC CLOVES, FINELY CHOPPED

¾ TEASPOON FINE SALT

TWO 15-OUNCE CANS BLACK BEANS, DRAINED AND RINSED

¾ CUP WATER

FOR THE BURRITO:

6 EGGS

NEW MEXICAN ROASTED GREEN CHILE SAUCE (PAGE 35)

FINE SALT

FRESHLY GROUND PEPPER

1 TABLESPOON UNSALTED BUTTER

½ CUP GRATED MONTEREY JACK CHEESE

SIX 8-INCH FLOUR TORTILLAS, WARMED

To make the beans:

1. In a medium frying pan over medium heat, heat the oil until shimmering. Add the onion, garlic, and salt and cook, stirring occasionally, until the onions are soft and just beginning to brown, about 5 minutes.

continued ▶

2. Add one-third of the beans and mash completely with the back of a spoon or a potato masher. Add another third of the beans and mash completely, stirring occasionally. Add the remaining third of the beans and mash, leaving about half of the beans intact.

3. Continue cooking, stirring constantly, until the bean starches begin to coat the bottom of the pan and turn golden brown, about 3 minutes. Add the water, bring to a simmer, and cook, stirring and scraping the bottom of the pan to incorporate the water and heat the beans through, about 2 minutes. (The beans will thicken as they cool, so be sure to add all of the water.)

To make the burrito:

1. In a medium bowl, whisk together the eggs and 2 tablespoons of the chile sauce. Season with salt and pepper.

2. In a medium nonstick frying pan over medium-low heat, melt the butter. Pour in the eggs and let sit undisturbed until the eggs just start to set around the edges, about 1½ to 2 minutes. Using a rubber spatula, push the eggs from the edges into the center. Let sit again for about 30 seconds, then repeat, pushing the eggs from the edges into the center every 30 seconds until just set. Remove the pan from the heat and stir in the cheese.

3. Place the tortillas on a work surface. Spoon an even amount of beans onto the lower third of each tortilla, leaving a 1-inch border. Divide the eggs over the beans, and spoon a tablespoon or two of chile sauce over the eggs.

4. Fold the sides of the tortilla in. Then hold the folds in place and roll the entire tortilla horizontally up from the bottom to the top. Turn the burrito so that the seam faces down, and repeat rolling the remaining burritos. Serve with the remaining chile sauce.

Grilled Chili and Cocoa–Rubbed Flank Steak with New Mexican Red Sauce

YIELD: 4 SERVINGS

Make sure to let the steak sit with the rub on it for at least 30 minutes so the dried spices can rehydrate and flavor the steak. Or if possible, let it sit overnight for even more flavor.

1 TABLESPOON CHILI POWDER

1 TABLESPOON NATURAL UNSWEETENED COCOA POWDER

1 TABLESPOON PACKED DARK BROWN SUGAR

2 TEASPOONS FINE SALT

½ TEASPOON FRESHLY GROUND PEPPER

1 TEASPOON GROUND CUMIN

1 TEASPOON GARLIC POWDER

ONE 1½- TO 2-POUND FLANK STEAK, TRIMMED OF FAT
    AND SILVER SKIN

1 TABLESPOON VEGETABLE OIL

NEW MEXICAN RED SAUCE (PAGE 36)

1. In a small bowl, mix together the chili powder, cocoa, sugar, salt, pepper, cumin, and garlic powder. Pat the steak dry with paper towels. Using your hands, rub the oil all over the steak and evenly coat with the spice mix. Place the steak on a large plate or baking sheet, and let sit at room temperature for 30 minutes or cover and refrigerate for up to 24 hours.

continued ▶

2. Heat an outdoor grill to high (about 450°F to 550°F). Place the steak on the grill, cover the grill, and cook until grill marks appear on the bottom, about 5 to 6 minutes. Flip the steak, cover the grill, and continue to cook until grill marks appear on the bottom and an instant-read thermometer inserted into the middle of the steak registers 125°F to 130°F for medium-rare, about 5 to 6 minutes more. Transfer to a cutting board and let rest for 10 to 15 minutes before thinly slicing the steak against the grain. Serve with New Mexican Red Sauce.

Carnitas Tacos with Pastor Salsa

YIELD: 8 TO 10 TACOS

"Carnitas" may sound exotic, but this recipe is quite easy to make. Just gather a few ingredients and let the pork cook until tender. Make sure to let the meat fry in the rendered fat so you have crispy bits of pork in your tacos.

3 FRESH MARJORAM SPRIGS

2 GARLIC CLOVES, PEELED AND SMASHED

1 TABLESPOON CORIANDER SEEDS

1 BAY LEAF

1 WHITE ONION, PEELED AND QUARTERED

1 TEASPOON FINE SALT

3 POUNDS UNTRIMMED BONELESS PORK SHOULDER, CUT INTO 2-INCH CUBES

WATER

CORN OR FLOUR TORTILLAS

GUACAMOLE

PASTOR SALSA (PAGE 45)

1. In a small piece of cheesecloth, place the marjoram, garlic, coriander, and bay leaf. Fold it into a bundle and tie it tightly with butcher's twine. Place the bundle in a Dutch oven or large, heavy-bottomed pot. Add the onion and salt. Place the pork in a single layer and add enough water to just cover the meat. Bring to a simmer over medium heat. Using a large spoon, skim off the foam that floats to the surface. Simmer (adjusting the heat as necessary to keep it at a simmer), skimming the surface and

continued ▶

turning the pork pieces occasionally, until the meat is tender and just beginning to shred apart, about 2½ hours.

2. Remove and discard the herb packet and onion. Increase the heat to medium-high and cook until the remaining water evaporates and just the rendered fat coats the bottom of the pan. Reduce the heat to low and let the meat fry in the fat, turning occasionally, until browned all over, about 20 minutes. Remove and discard any large pieces of unrendered fat.

3. To serve, warm the tortillas by heating a medium frying pan over medium-high heat. Add 1 tortilla at a time, flipping to warm both sides. Wrap the warm tortillas in a clean dishcloth. Break up some of the carnitas and place them on the warm tortilla. Top with some of the guacamole and Pastor Salsa.

Crunchy Fish Tostadas with Cabbage Slaw Verde

YIELD: 4 SERVINGS

The marinade and dressing for the fish and cabbage slaw are surprisingly simple to put together. The crunchy tostadas add texture, but you can use soft tortillas, too.

FISH

¼ TEASPOON GROUND CUMIN

¼ TEASPOON GARLIC POWDER

¼ TEASPOON CHILI POWDER

1 POUND FIRM WHITE FISH, SUCH AS SNAPPER, COD, TILAPIA, OR MAHI MAHI

2 LIMES, HALVED

2 TABLESPOONS VEGETABLE OIL

FINE SALT

FRESHLY GROUND PEPPER

CABBAGE SLAW

½ SMALL HEAD OF GREEN OR RED CABBAGE, CORED AND THINLY SLICED

¼ CUP CHOPPED RED ONION

¼ CUP COARSELY CHOPPED FRESH CILANTRO

4 TOSTADA SHELLS

1 AVOCADO, CUT INTO THIN SLICES

SMOOTH SALSA VERDE (PAGE 40)

continued ▶

To make the fish:

1. In a small bowl, stir together the cumin, garlic, and chili powder. Place the fish in a nonreactive dish and sprinkle both sides with the spice mix. Squeeze one of the lime halves over the fish and drizzle with 1 tablespoon of the oil. Season with salt and pepper and turn the fish in the marinade until evenly coated. Refrigerate for 15 minutes.

2. Brush the grates of a grill pan or outdoor grill with oil and heat over medium-high heat (about 375°F to 450°F).

3. Place the fish on the grill and cook undisturbed until the underside is white and opaque, about 3 minutes. Flip and grill the other side until white and opaque, about 2 to 3 minutes more. (It's okay if the fish breaks apart while flipping.) Transfer the fish to a clean plate and break into large pieces.

To make the cabbage slaw:

In a large bowl, combine the cabbage, onion, and cilantro, and squeeze one of the lime halves over the misture. Drizzle in the remaining tablespoon of oil, season with salt and pepper, and toss to combine. Slice the remaining lime halves into wedges; set aside.

To make the tostadas:

To construct each tostada, place one-quarter of the cabbage on one tostada shell, then one-quarter of the fish, and top with one-quarter of the avocado. Drizzle with some of the Salsa Verde, and serve with lime wedges and extra Salsa Verde on the side. Repeat to make each tostada.

Salvadoran Cheese and Bean Papusas with Salsa Roja

YIELD: 6 PAPUSAS

Check out Latin markets to find the masa harina and queso fresco. Once you master the technique of filling papusas (little balls of dough), try adding other kinds of cheese, cooked meat, or vegetables.

3 CUPS MASA HARINA

1⅔ CUPS WARM WATER

½ TEASPOON FINE SALT

1 CUP REFRIED BEANS

1½ CUPS CRUMBLED QUESO FRESCO

VEGETABLE OIL FOR COATING THE SKILLET

SALVADORAN SALSA ROJA (PAGE 47)

1. In a large bowl, mix together the masa harina, water, and salt until it forms a soft dough. Add more water 1 tablespoon at a time if necessary until the dough doesn't crack around the edges when flattened. Cover the bowl with plastic wrap and let sit for 15 minutes.

2. Put the refried beans in a food processor fitted with the blade attachment and process until very smooth.

3. Divide the dough into six pieces and roll each piece into a ball. Using your finger, make an indentation in the center of each ball. Place 1 tablespoon of cheese and 1 tablespoon of beans into the indentation.

continued ▶

Salvadoran Cheese and Bean Papusas with Salsa Roja *continued* ▶

Carefully wrap the dough around the filling to seal. Flatten the balls into ¼-inch-thick disks, being careful to keep the filling from leaking out.

4. Using a paper towel, thinly coat the surface of a large cast iron skillet with oil. Heat the skillet over medium heat, and place two of the papusas in the skillet. Cook about 2 to 3 minutes per side or until golden brown on the bottom. Serve warm with Salsa Roja.

Grilled Corn with Belizean Carrot-Orange Hot Sauce

YIELD: 6 SERVINGS

Corn prepared this way is common in Mexico, but adding the zing of Belizean hot sauce adds another level of flavor that pairs well with the sweet corn and cheese.

6 TABLESPOONS MAYONNAISE

2 TABLESPOONS BELIZEAN CARROT-ORANGE HOT SAUCE (PAGE 50)

1 GARLIC CLOVE, FINELY CHOPPED

½ TEASPOON FINE SALT

¾ CUP (ABOUT 4 OUNCES) CRUMBLED COTIJA CHEESE

6 EARS CORN, HUSKS ON

1 LIME, CUT INTO 6 WEDGES

1. In a small bowl, stir together the mayonnaise, hot sauce, garlic, and salt. Put the cheese in a long shallow dish.

2. Heat the grill to medium-high (about 375°F to 450°F). Peel back the husks of the corn just over halfway; remove as much silk as you can without pulling the husks off completely, and pull the husks back up.

3. Place the corn on the grill and close the lid. Roll the corn a quarter turn every 10 minutes until the husks are charred and starting to peel back from the corn, about 35 minutes total. Remove the corn from the grill and set aside until cool enough to handle.

4. Peel back the husks without detaching, turning them inside out so they form a handle. Brush the corn with a thin layer of the mayonnaise mixture, roll the cobs in the crumbled cheese, and serve. Serve with the lime wedges on the side for squeezing over the corn.

CHAPTER FIVE

LOUISIANA

Basic Louisiana Hot Red Pepper Sauce

YIELD: 3 CUPS

You can use this hot sauce right away, but aging it develops its flavor.

1 POUND RED JALAPEÑO CHILES, STEMMED
2 CUPS DISTILLED WHITE VINEGAR
2 TEASPOONS FINE SALT

1. In a large saucepan over high heat, bring the chiles, vinegar, and salt to a simmer. Reduce the heat to medium and let simmer until the chiles are soft, about 5 minutes more.

2. Transfer the mixture to a blender. Remove the small cap in the blender lid, place the lid on the blender, and cover the hole with a kitchen towel. Blend until smooth, stopping and scraping down the sides of the blender with a rubber spatula if necessary. Transfer to an airtight container and refrigerate 2 weeks before using. Will keep in the refrigerator for up to 4 months.

Red Hot Sauce in the Style of Frank's

YIELD: 2 CUPS

Mix this hot sauce with some melted butter and toss with fried, broiled, or grilled chicken wings for the classic bar snack.

1 TABLESPOON VEGETABLE OIL

10 OUNCES TABASCO OR RED SERRANO CHILES, STEMMED AND CUT INTO ⅛-INCH-THICK SLICES

5 GARLIC CLOVES, FINELY CHOPPED

¾ CUP CHOPPED YELLOW ONION

¾ TEASPOON FINE SALT

2 CUPS WATER

1 CUP DISTILLED WHITE VINEGAR

1. In a medium saucepan, heat the oil over high heat. Add the chiles, garlic, onion, and salt and cook, stirring occasionally, for 4 minutes. Add the water and continue to cook, stirring occasionally, until almost all of the water has evaporated and the chiles are soft, about 20 minutes.

2. Transfer the mixture to a food processor fitted with the blade attachment and process until smooth. With the processor running, pour in the vinegar and process until evenly incorporated.

3. Place a mesh sieve over a measuring cup and strain the mixture. Discard the solids. Season with salt if necessary. Transfer to an airtight container and refrigerate for 2 weeks before using. Will keep in the refrigerator for up to 6 months.

Easy Aged Pepper Mash

YIELD: 3 CUPS

Fermenting the mashed peppers gives this an extra layer of flavor, so be patient and make sure to let the mash sit for at least a week. When it's ready, use it as a base to make other sauces like Texas Pete-Style Hot Sauce (page 68) or Sriracha (page 112).

2 POUNDS RED JALAPEÑO CHILES
¼ CUP FINE KOSHER SALT
1 CUP PURIFIED WATER
2 TABLESPOONS WHITE WINE VINEGAR

1. Set three chiles aside. Spread out the remaining chiles on a baking sheet and put them in a sunny spot for 2 days, or until soft and wrinkled.

2. Stem the softened chiles, slice them lengthwise, and put them in a large bowl. Sprinkle with the salt. Using a potato masher, smash the chiles until only large chunks remain. Set aside at room temperature uncovered for 24 hours.

3. Transfer the chiles and any liquid in the bowl to a 1-quart mason jar with a two-piece lid. Put any mashed chiles that don't fit into a separate container for later use. Pour the water into the jar, loosely fit the lid, and place the jar on a plate. Let the mixture sit at room temperature until it begins to fizz over and the peppers shrink, about 1 or 2 days.

4. Add the leftover reserved mashed chiles to the jar. Place the three reserved whole chiles at the top of the jar to make sure the mashed chiles are submerged under the liquid. Loosely replace the lid and let sit at room temperature to ferment for at least 1 week and up to 2 weeks. (You may need to add more purified water to the jar to keep the chiles submerged.)

5. Wearing food handler's gloves, remove the whole chiles from the jar and discard. Remove the seeds from the mashed chiles and transfer to a food processor fitted with a blade attachment.

6. Process the chiles. Add the vinegar and any leftover liquid from the jar. Process until smooth. Transfer to an airtight container and refrigerate for up to 4 months. (The mash will continue to ferment and fizz a bit.)

Texas Pete–Style Hot Sauce

YIELD: 2½ CUPS

Depending on your taste, you can use a bit less vinegar than called for here. When it's ready, use this sauce to cut through creamy dishes like shrimp and grits, or clam chowder.

1⅓ CUPS DISTILLED WHITE VINEGAR
1 CUP EASY AGED PEPPER MASH (PAGE 66)

1. In a blender, combine the vinegar and mash, and blend until smooth.

2. Put a mesh strainer over a large measuring cup and strain the mixture, pushing on the solids with a rubber spatula. Scrape the sauce clinging to the bottom of the strainer into the measuring cup. Discard the solids. Transfer to an airtight container and refrigerate for up to 4 months.

Crystal-Style Sauce

YIELD: 1⅔ CUPS

This hot sauce is similar to Texas Pete but uses much less vinegar, which allows the flavor of the chiles to come through. It is especially tasty on pepperoni pizza.

⅔ CUP DISTILLED WHITE VINEGAR
1 CUP EASY AGED PEPPER MASH (PAGE 66)

1. In a blender, combine the vinegar and mash, and blend until smooth.

2. Put a mesh strainer over a large measuring cup and strain the mixture, pushing on the solids with a rubber spatula. Scrape the sauce clinging to the bottom of the strainer into the measuring cup. Discard the solids. Transfer to an airtight container and refrigerate up to 4 months.

Tabasco-Style Sauce

YIELD: 2 CUPS

Like Basic Louisiana Hot Red Pepper Sauce (page 64), this simple mixture of chiles, vinegar, and salt benefits from spending time aging in the refrigerator. Using a mixture of cayenne and Tabasco chiles gives it an authentic flavor.

12 OUNCES CAYENNE OR TABASCO CHILES, STEMMED
12 OUNCES DISTILLED WHITE VINEGAR
1½ TEASPOONS FINE SALT

1. In a large saucepan over high heat, bring the chiles, vinegar, and salt to a simmer. Reduce the heat to medium and let simmer until soft, about 5 minutes more.

2. Transfer the mixture to a blender. Remove the small cap in the blender lid, place the lid on the blender, and cover the hole with a kitchen towel. Blend until smooth, stopping and scraping the sides of the blender with a rubber spatula if necessary. Transfer to an airtight container and refrigerate for 2 weeks before using. Will keep in the refrigerator for up to 4 months.

Herbed Louisiana Hot Pepper Sauce

YIELD: 2 CUPS

With a little basil, oregano, and celery seed, this herbed sauce makes a delicious addition to scalloped potatoes or succotash.

1½ POUNDS RED SERRANO CHILES
5 GARLIC CLOVES, CHOPPED
1¼ TEASPOONS FINELY CHOPPED FRESH BASIL
1¼ TEASPOONS FINELY CHOPPED FRESH OREGANO
½ TEASPOON CELERY SEEDS
½ TEASPOON FINE SALT
¼ TEASPOON FRESHLY GROUND PEPPER
1¼ CUPS DISTILLED WHITE VINEGAR

1. Preheat the oven to broil and arrange a rack on the upper third. Arrange the chiles in a singe layer on a baking sheet and broil, turning the chiles as the skins begin to blister and turn black all over, about 6 to 8 minutes total. Transfer the chiles to a large bowl, cover with plastic wrap, and let sit for 10 minutes.

2. Stem and peel the chiles (keep the seeds intact). In a food processor fitted with the blade attachment, combine the chiles, garlic, basil, oregano, celery seeds, salt, and pepper. With the motor running, slowly add the vinegar and process until smooth.

3. Place a mesh sieve over a measuring cup and strain the sauce, pushing on the solids with a rubber spatula. Scrape the sauce clinging to the bottom of the strainer into the measuring cup. Discard the solids. Transfer to an airtight container and refrigerate. The hot sauce will keep in the refrigerator for up to 1 month.

Garlicky Hot Red Pepper Sauce

YIELD: 3 CUPS

Depending on your love for garlic, add as much or as little as you like. This hot sauce is a great addition to a Bloody Mary.

1 POUND RED CHILES, SUCH AS JALAPEÑOS, SERRANOS,
   OR CAYENNE, STEMMED
6 GARLIC CLOVES
2 CUPS DISTILLED WHITE VINEGAR
2 TEASPOONS FINE SALT

1. In a large saucepan over high heat, bring the chiles, garlic, vinegar, and salt to a simmer. Reduce the heat to medium and let simmer until the chiles are soft, about 5 minutes more.

2. Transfer the mixture to a blender. Remove the small cap in the blender lid, place the lid on the blender, and cover the hole with a kitchen towel. Blend until smooth, stopping and scraping the sides of the blender with a rubber spatula if necessary. Transfer to an airtight container and refrigerate for 2 weeks before using. This recipe will keep in the refrigerator for up to 4 months.

Green Louisiana Hot Pepper Sauce

YIELD: 3 CUPS

Using green chiles adds a vegetal flavor to this hot sauce. Mix it into a creamy salad dressing to drizzle over greens, or use it in a vinaigrette to pour over steamed green beans.

1 POUND GREEN CHILES, SUCH AS JALAPEÑOS OR SERRANOS
2 GARLIC CLOVES
¼ CUP CHOPPED YELLOW ONION
½ TEASPOON DRIED OREGANO
2 CUPS DISTILLED WHITE VINEGAR
2 TEASPOONS FINE SALT

1. In a large saucepan over high heat, bring the chiles, garlic, onion, oregano, vinegar, and salt to a simmer. Reduce the heat to medium and let simmer until the chiles are soft, about 5 minutes more.

2. Transfer the mixture to a blender. Remove the small cap in the blender lid, place the lid on the blender, and cover the hole with a kitchen towel. Blend until smooth, stopping and scraping down the sides of the blender with a rubber spatula if necessary. Transfer to an airtight container and refrigerate for 2 weeks before using. It will keep in the refrigerator for up to 4 months.

Cajun Barbecue Sauce

YIELD: ABOUT 2 CUPS

Creole mustard gives this sauce an extra kick of flavor, but if you can't find Creole mustard, any whole-grain mustard will work. This sauce is especially good with grilled shrimp or on a chicken sandwich.

1 TABLESPOON VEGETABLE OIL

½ CUP FINELY CHOPPED RED ONION

1 CUP KETCHUP

1 CUP WATER

¼ CUP PACKED DARK-BROWN SUGAR

¼ CUP WORCESTERSHIRE SAUCE

2 TABLESPOONS RED WINE VINEGAR

1 TABLESPOON CHILI POWDER

1 TABLESPOON CREOLE MUSTARD

1 TEASPOON CAYENNE PEPPER

½ TEASPOON FINE SALT

1. In a medium saucepan over medium heat, heat the oil. Add the onion and cook, stirring occasionally until softened, about 5 minutes.

2. Add the remaining ingredients, stir to combine, and bring to a simmer. Reduce the heat to low and simmer, stirring often, for 10 to 15 minutes or until thickened and reduced to about 2 cups. The sauce can be used immediately or stored in an airtight container in the refrigerator for up to 1 week.

Chickasaw Hot Sauce

YIELD: ABOUT 2½ CUPS

Named after the indigenous people of the Southeastern Woodlands, this sauce gets a Southern-inspired flavor from Louisiana-style hot sauce.

2 CUPS KETCHUP

1 CUP WATER

¾ CUP DARK MOLASSES

2 TABLESPOONS CIDER VINEGAR

2 TABLESPOONS TEXAS PETE–STYLE, CRYSTAL-STYLE,
    OR TABASCO-STYLE HOT SAUCE (PAGES 68, 69, 70)

4 TEASPOONS WORCESTERSHIRE SAUCE

2 TABLESPOONS FRESHLY SQUEEZED LEMON JUICE

½ CUP CHOPPED YELLOW ONION

2 GARLIC CLOVES, FINELY CHOPPED

¼ CUP LIGHT BROWN SUGAR

1 TEASPOON CAYENNE PEPPER

2 TEASPOONS GROUND GINGER

In a large saucepan over medium heat, combine all of the ingredients and bring to a boil. Reduce the heat to simmer. Cook until thickened and reduced to about 2½ cups. Use immediately or store in an airtight container in the refrigerator for 1 week.

Spicy New Orleans Cocktail Sauce

YIELD: 1¾ CUPS

Cocktail sauce is a natural accompaniment to cold cooked shrimp, but try this spicy sauce on freshly shucked oysters, too.

1½ CUPS KETCHUP

1 TABLESPOON WORCESTERSHIRE SAUCE

¼ CUP PREPARED HORSERADISH

2 TEASPOONS TEXAS PETE–STYLE, CRYSTAL-STYLE,
    OR TABASCO-STYLE HOT SAUCE (PAGES 68, 69, 70)

1 TEASPOON FRESHLY SQUEEZED LEMON JUICE

¼ TEASPOON FRESHLY GROUND PEPPER, PLUS MORE TO TASTE

In a medium bowl, stir together all of the ingredients. Season with additional pepper as needed. Cover the bowl with plastic wrap and chill until ready to serve. This sauce will keep in the refrigerator for up to 4 days.

Smothered Over-Easy Eggs on Biscuits with Sausage Gravy

YIELD: 4 SERVINGS

To make this rustic breakfast fancy enough to serve for brunch, change it to poached eggs with a slice of country ham on the biscuit. A side of home fries with extra hot sauce won't hurt, either.

6 TABLESPOONS UNSALTED BUTTER

12 OUNCES UNCOOKED BREAKFAST SAUSAGE, CASINGS REMOVED

⅓ CUP ALL-PURPOSE FLOUR

½ TEASPOON FINE SALT

½ TEASPOON FRESHLY GROUND PEPPER

4 CUPS MILK (NOT NONFAT)

¼ CUP GARLICKY HOT RED PEPPER SAUCE (PAGE 72),
     PLUS EXTRA FOR SERVING

8 EGGS

8 BISCUITS, HOMEMADE OR STORE-BOUGHT, SPLIT

1. In a large frying pan over medium-high heat, melt 3 tablespoons of the butter. Add the sausage and cook, breaking it up into smaller pieces with a wooden spoon, until browned, about 5 minutes.

2. Reduce the heat to medium. Sprinkle the sausage with the flour, salt, and pepper. Cook, stirring frequently, until the flour smells toasted, about 1 minute. Gradually stir in the milk, scraping up any browned bits from the bottom of the pan. Add the hot sauce and bring to a simmer, stirring often, until the mixture has thickened slightly, about

continued ▶

1 minute. The gravy will continue to thicken as it sits. Season with additional salt and pepper, if necessary. Keep warm.

3. In a large nonstick frying pan over medium-low heat, melt the remaining 3 tablespoons butter. Crack four eggs into the pan, season with salt and pepper, and let cook undisturbed until the tops of the eggs are almost completely opaque, about 3 to 4 minutes. Using a flat spatula, flip the eggs and continue to cook until the whites are completely set but the yolks are still runny, about 1 minute more. Repeat with the remaining four eggs.

4. Place four biscuit halves on each plate and place one egg over two of the halves. Smother with gravy and serve immediately with extra hot sauce.

Hot Sauce and Buttermilk Fried Chicken

YIELD: 4 SERVINGS

Buttermilk makes this chicken extra moist; the longer it sits in the hot sauce–spiked marinade, the more flavor it gets.

4 CUPS BUTTERMILK

¼ CUP RED HOT SAUCE IN THE STYLE OF FRANK'S (PAGE 65),
   PLUS EXTRA FOR SERVING

1 TEASPOON FINE SALT

¼ TEASPOON DRIED THYME

½ TEASPOON FRESHLY GROUND PEPPER

2 POUNDS CHICKEN DRUMSTICKS

4 CUPS VEGETABLE OIL

1 CUP ALL-PURPOSE FLOUR

1. In a resealable plastic bag, combine the buttermilk, hot sauce, salt, thyme, and pepper. Add the chicken, seal the bag, and turn to coat the chicken. Let marinate 30 minutes at room temperature or refrigerate overnight. (If you refrigerate the chicken overnight, let it sit at room temperature for 30 minutes before frying.)

2. In a large, heavy-bottomed pot or Dutch oven, heat the oil over medium-low heat until it reaches between 350°F and 360°F on a deep-frying thermometer, about 20 minutes. (There should be about 2 to 3 inches of oil in the pan.) Set a wire rack over a baking sheet and set it aside.

continued ▶

3. When the oil is ready, place the flour in a shallow dish and season with salt and pepper. Remove half of the drumsticks from the buttermilk, letting the excess liquid drip off. Coat the chicken in the flour mixture, shaking off the excess. Carefully lay the pieces in the oil and fry until cooked through and golden brown, flipping halfway through, about 20 minutes total. An instant-read thermometer inserted into the thickest part of the drumstick should read 160°F to 165°F. Place the drumsticks on the wire. Repeat with the remaining chicken. Serve immediately with extra hot sauce.

Deviled Ham with Crostini

YIELD: 8 APPETIZER SERVINGS

Serve this old-school dish as an appetizer in an attractive ramekin like pâté, or spread it on Pullman bread to make finger sandwiches.

1 FRENCH BAGUETTE, CUT ON THE BIAS INTO ¼-INCH-THICK SLICES
2 TABLESPOONS OLIVE OIL
FINE SALT
FRESHLY GROUND PEPPER
½ CUP MAYONNAISE
¼ CUP DILL PICKLE RELISH
1 TABLESPOON DIJON MUSTARD
1 TABLESPOON GREEN LOUISIANA HOT PEPPER SAUCE (PAGE 73)
1 TEASPOON WORCESTERSHIRE SAUCE
1 POUND SMOKED HAM, CUT INTO 1-INCH CHUNKS
¼ CUP COARSELY CHOPPED YELLOW ONION

1. Preheat the oven to 350°F and arrange a rack in the middle. Place the bread slices on a baking sheet, lightly brush them with the oil, and season with salt and pepper. Bake until golden brown, about 10 to 12 minutes. Transfer to a wire rack to cool. The crostini can be stored in an airtight container at room temperature for up to 2 days.

2. In a large bowl, combine the mayonnaise, relish, mustard, hot sauce, and Worcestershire sauce; set aside. Put the ham in the bowl of a food processor fitted with the blade attachment and process until coarsely chopped, about 10 seconds. Add the onion and process, stopping to scrape down the sides of the bowl with a rubber spatula as needed, until a thick paste forms, about 1 minute. Transfer the ham mixture to the bowl with the mayonnaise mixture and stir until evenly combined. Serve immediately with the crostini or refrigerate in an airtight container for up to 3 days.

Panfried Catfish Sandwich with Spicy Mayo

YIELD: 4 SANDWICHES

This sandwich is the perfect balance of crunchy, crisp, and smooth, while the mayo gives it a hot bite.

SPICY MAYO

1 CUP MAYONNAISE

1 TABLESPOON DIJON MUSTARD

1 TABLESPOON FRESHLY SQUEEZED LEMON JUICE

1 TABLESPOON CRYSTAL-STYLE OR TABASCO-STYLE HOT SAUCE
(PAGES 69–70), PLUS EXTRA FOR SERVING

2 TEASPOONS FINELY CHOPPED CAPERS

2 TEASPOONS FINELY CHOPPED SHALLOT

1 TEASPOON FINELY CHOPPED ITALIAN PARSLEY LEAVES

1 TEASPOON WORCESTERSHIRE SAUCE

½ TEASPOON FRESHLY GROUND PEPPER

SANDWICHES

½ CUP FINELY GROUND YELLOW CORNMEAL

½ CUP FLOUR

2 TEASPOONS GROUND CAYENNE PEPPER

1 TEASPOON FINE SALT

1 TEASPOON FRESHLY GROUND PEPPER

4 CUPS VEGETABLE OIL

2 POUNDS CATFISH FILLETS, CUT IN HALF LENGTHWISE

4 HOAGIE ROLLS, SPLIT IN HALF AND TOASTED

½ HEAD ICEBERG LETTUCE, CUT INTO VERY THIN STRIPS

2 RIPE TOMATOES, CUT INTO ¼-INCH-THICK SLICES AND SEASONED
WITH SALT

To make the mayo:

In a medium bowl, combine all of the ingredients. Cover and refrigerate until ready to use.

To make the sandwiches:

1. In a shallow dish, whisk together the cornmeal, flour, cayenne, salt, and pepper. In a 12-inch cast-iron skillet, heat the vegetable oil over medium heat until it reaches between 350°F and 360°F on a deep-frying thermometer, about 20 minutes (there should be about 2 inches of oil). Line a baking sheet with several layers of paper towels and fit it with a wire rack; set aside.

2. Use a paper towel to pat the fish dry. Season on all sides with salt and pepper, and coat with the cornmeal mixture. Tap the fish pieces lightly to shake off any excess coating.

3. Fry the fish in three to four batches, turning once, until deep golden brown and crisp on the outside with a flaky interior, about 6 minutes total. Using a slotted spatula, transfer the fish to the prepared baking sheet and immediately season with salt.

4. Spread 3 tablespoons of the mayo on each roll to coat both cut sides. Place one-quarter of the lettuce on the bread, and top with one-quarter of the tomato slices and one-quarter of the fish pieces. Close the sandwiches and serve immediately with extra hot sauce.

Steamed Shrimp with Spicy New Orleans Cocktail Sauce

YIELD: 6 TO 8 SERVINGS

Cajun or Creole seasoning is a mixture of oregano, paprika, cayenne, and other spices. It adds an extra zing to the shrimp. However, you can steam the shrimp without the seasoning, or switch it up and try Old Bay instead.

2 POUNDS EXTRA-LARGE SHRIMP

2 TEASPOONS CAJUN OR CREOLE SEASONING

12 OUNCES BEER

3 CLOVES GARLIC, PEELED AND CRUSHED

SPICY NEW ORLEANS COCKTAIL SAUCE (PAGE 76)

1. In a large bowl, toss the shrimp with the seasoning; set aside.

2. In the base pot of a steamer over medium heat, bring the beer and garlic to a simmer. Insert the steamer basket and place the shrimp inside it. Cover and steam until the shrimp are firm and opaque, about 5 minutes, stirring once to ensure even cooking. Remove the basket with the shrimp and transfer to a serving dish. Serve with Spicy New Orleans Cocktail Sauce for dipping.

Oyster and Andouille Stew

YIELD: 4 SERVINGS

This creamy soup benefits from the addition of vinegary Louisiana Hot Red Pepper Sauce. Make sure to heat the oysters until just cooked through. The bread is great for dunking and for mopping up the last bits in the bowl. Jarred freshly shucked oysters are typically available at any good fish market, but use discretion—make sure they are impeccably fresh.

TWO 16-OUNCE JARS FRESHLY SHUCKED OYSTERS

1¼ CUPS COLD WATER

½ CUP (1 STICK) UNSALTED BUTTER

4 OUNCES ANDOUILLE SAUSAGE, CUT INTO ¼-INCH DICE

1 CUP FINELY CHOPPED CELERY

¼ TEASPOON WHITE PEPPER

¼ TEASPOON FINE SALT

½ CUP FINELY CHOPPED GREEN ONION (WHITE AND
    LIGHT GREEN PARTS)

1 TABLESPOON BASIC LOUISIANA HOT RED PEPPER SAUCE (PAGE 64)

2 CUPS HEAVY CREAM

CRUSTY BREAD (OPTIONAL)

1. In a large bowl, combine the oysters and the water. Refrigerate for 1 hour. Strain the oysters, reserving the liquid. Set both the oysters and liquid aside.

2. In a large frying pan over medium heat, melt the butter. Add the sausage. Cook, stirring often, until just beginning to brown, about 5 minutes. Add the celery, pepper, and salt. Cook, stirring occasionally, until the celery softens slightly, about 3 minutes. Increase the heat to

continued ▶

Oyster and Andouille Stew *continued* ▶

high, add ¾ cup of the reserved oyster liquid, and cook while constantly shaking the pan for 1 minute. Add the remaining ½ cup oyster liquid and cook for 1 minute more.

3. Stir in the green onion and hot sauce. Slowly whisk in the cream and bring to a boil while still whisking. Add the oysters and cook, whisking constantly, just until the oysters curl, about 2 to 4 minutes. Serve immediately with extra hot sauce and crusty bread.

CHAPTER SIX

WEST INDIES AND THE CARIBBEAN

Sauce Ti Malice

Bermudan Pepper Sherry

Caribbean-Style Hot Sauce

Puerto Rican Pique

Jamaican Scotch Bonnet
Pepper Sauce

Escabeche (Pickled Peppers)

Papaya Chile Hot Sauce

Jerk Sauce

Hot Curried Caribbean Sauce

Sauce Chien

Spicy Caribbean Sweet Potato Stew

Caribbean Black Beans
and Plantains

Spice-Rubbed Rack of Lamb

Jerk-Marinated Barbecue Chicken

Pan-Seared Halibut with
Sauce Chien

Sauce Ti Malice

YIELD: ABOUT 2 CUPS

A mischievous character in Haitian folklore, Ti Malice is said to have created this fiery sauce to deter his freeloading friend, Bouki, from always showing up at mealtime. He hoped Bouki would put the hot sauce on his food, be repelled by the spice, and never return. Unfortunately, Bouki loved it and told everyone about Ti Malice's sauce.

1 TABLESPOON OLIVE OIL

1 CUP CHOPPED YELLOW ONION

1 GARLIC CLOVE, SMASHED

2 SCOTCH BONNET OR HABANERO CHILES, STEMMED AND
    FINELY CHOPPED

½ TEASPOON FINE SALT

¼ TEASPOON FRESHLY GROUND PEPPER

¾ CUP WATER

½ CUP FRESHLY SQUEEZED LEMON JUICE

1. In a large frying pan over medium heat, heat the oil. Add the onion and garlic and cook, stirring occasionally, until the onions have softened, about 5 minutes. Reduce the heat to low and add the chiles, salt, and pepper; stir to combine. Cover and cook until the chiles are soft, about 10 minutes.

2. Turn off the heat and stir in the water and lemon juice. Transfer the mixture to a blender. Remove the small cap in the blender lid, place the lid on the blender, and cover the hole with a kitchen towel. Blend until smooth, stopping and scraping down the sides of the blender with a rubber spatula if necessary. Transfer to an airtight container and store in the refrigerator for a few hours before serving. The sauce will keep in the refrigerator for up to 1 week.

Bermudan Pepper Sherry

YIELD: ONE 750 ML BOTTLE

Cutting a slit in the sides of each one of these tiny chiles is a tedious task, but doing so allows the heat from the pepper to infuse with the sherry.

ONE 750 ML BOTTLE DRY OR SWEET SHERRY
½ CUP PIQUÍN CHILES, OR OTHER CHILES SMALL ENOUGH TO FIT
    THROUGH THE BOTTLE MOUTH

1. Using a sharp knife, make a small slit in the side of each chile.

2. Remove ½ cup of the sherry and save for another use. Drop the chiles into the bottle. Seal tightly and let the sherry age for at least 1 week before using.

Caribbean-Style Hot Sauce

YIELD: ABOUT 2 CUPS

Caribbean hot sauces are known for their mix of fruit and heat from the Scotch bonnet chile. In this recipe, mango is added to give the sauce a smooth and silky consistency.

6 SCOTCH BONNET OR HABANERO CHILES, STEMMED

2 GARLIC CLOVES, PEELED

1 SHALLOT, COARSELY CHOPPED

1 CUP CHOPPED RIPE MANGO

1 TABLESPOON FINELY CHOPPED GINGER

½ CUP FRESHLY SQUEEZED ORANGE JUICE

½ CUP FRESHLY SQUEEZED LIME JUICE

½ TEASPOON FINE SALT

1. Put all of the ingredients in a food processor fitted with the blade attachment and process until smooth. Transfer to a medium saucepan, place over high heat, and bring to a boil. Reduce the heat to medium and let simmer for 10 minutes.

2. Remove from the heat and let cool. Transfer to an airtight container. The sauce will keep in the refrigerator for up to 1 month.

Puerto Rican Pique

YIELD: ABOUT 3 CUPS

This concoction of spices, chiles, and vinegar is commonly seen on restaurant and kitchen tables all over Puerto Rico. If you can't find caballero chiles, customize using whatever chiles suit your taste!

1 CUP CABALLERO OR OTHER SMALL RED CHILES
4 GARLIC CLOVES, SLICED
2 BAY LEAVES
2 TEASPOONS BLACK PEPPERCORNS
½ TEASPOON DRIED OREGANO
⅛ TEASPOON FINE SALT
12 OUNCES APPLE CIDER VINEGAR
½ CUP PURIFIED WATER

In a 20-ounce bottle, combine the chiles, garlic, bay leaves, peppercorns, oregano, and salt. Pour in the vinegar using a funnel, and top with the water. Seal tightly and let sit in a cool place for at least 4 days before using. The sauce will keep in the refrigerator for up to 3 months.

Jamaican Scotch Bonnet Pepper Sauce

YIELD: ABOUT 2 CUPS

After blending, it may seem like the sieve is keeping all of the flavor, but the resulting sauce will have loads of chile flavor and be very spicy.

2 TABLESPOONS VEGETABLE OIL

1 YELLOW ONION, CHOPPED

6 CARROTS, CHOPPED

2 CHAYOTES, CHOPPED

10 WHOLE ALLSPICE BERRIES

3 GARLIC CLOVES

ONE 1-INCH PIECE GINGER, PEELED AND CUT CROSSWISE
    INTO ⅛-INCH-THICK SLICES

8 SCOTCH BONNET CHILES, STEMMED AND CHOPPED

½ CUP DISTILLED WHITE VINEGAR

1. In a large frying pan over medium heat, heat the oil. Add the onion and cook, stirring occasionally, until softened, about 10 minutes.

2. Add the carrots, chayotes, allspice, garlic, and ginger. Cook until the allspice is fragrant, about 5 minutes. Add the chiles and vinegar. Cook, stirring occasionally, until the chiles have softened, about 10 minutes.

3. Transfer the mixture to a blender. Remove the small cap in the blender lid, place the lid on the blender, and cover the hole with a kitchen towel. Blend until smooth, stopping and scraping down the sides of the blender with a rubber spatula if necessary.

4. Put a mesh sieve over a measuring cup and pour in the mixture. Let sit until all of the liquid drains from the solids. Discard the solids in the strainer. Transfer the liquid to an airtight container. The sauce will keep in the refrigerator for up to 1 month.

Escabeche (Pickled Peppers)

YIELD: TWO 16-OUNCE JARS

The liquid is great to drizzle over salad for a bit of heat, or add the hot pickled vegetables to your favorite meal. They make a great side.

1 TABLESPOON OLIVE OIL

1 WHITE ONION, CUT INTO ¼-INCH-THICK SLICES

3 GARLIC CLOVES, QUARTERED LENGTHWISE

5 CUPS WATER

8 OUNCES JALAPEÑO CHILES

1 CUP CARROTS, CUT CROSSWISE INTO ¼-INCH-THICK SLICES

1¼ CUPS DISTILLED WHITE VINEGAR

1 BAY LEAF

1 TABLESPOON FINE SALT

½ TEASPOON DRIED OREGANO

1. In a large pot over medium heat, heat the oil. Add the onion and garlic and cook, stirring occasionally, until the onion has softened, about 10 minutes.

2. Increase the heat to high, add the water, and bring to a boil. Add the chiles and carrots, and cook until just beginning to soften, about 5 minutes. Add 1 cup of the vinegar, bay leaf, salt, and oregano, and stir until the salt dissolves. Remove from the heat and let cool.

3. Using a slotted spoon, divide the vegetables between two clean 16-ounce jars. Add the remaining ¼ cup of vinegar to each jar, dividing it equally, and fill with the cooled cooking liquid. Seal tightly and refrigerate for up to 3 months.

Papaya Chile Hot Sauce

YIELD: ABOUT 3 CUPS

This medium hot sauce has a balance of sweet from the papaya and savory notes from the mustard, thyme, peppercorn, and allspice.

1 TABLESPOON VEGETABLE OIL

1 CUP CHOPPED WHITE ONION

3 WHOLE ALLSPICE BERRIES

5 BLACK PEPPERCORNS

1 TABLESPOON FINELY CHOPPED GINGER

1 TEASPOON DRIED MUSTARD

1 TEASPOON DRIED THYME

2 TABLESPOONS GRANULATED SUGAR

3 CUPS CHOPPED PAPAYA

3 SCOTCH BONNET OR HABANERO CHILES, STEMMED AND CHOPPED

½ CUP CIDER VINEGAR

¼ CUP FRESHLY SQUEEZED LIME JUICE

1. In a large saucepan over medium heat, heat the oil. Add the onion, allspice, peppercorns, ginger, mustard, and thyme. Cook, stirring occasionally, until the onions have softened, about 5 minutes. Add the sugar, papaya, and chiles and cook until the sugar dissolves. Add the vinegar and cook until the papaya is very soft, about 10 minutes.

2. Transfer the mixture to a blender and add the lime juice. Remove the small cap in the blender lid, place the lid on the blender, and cover the hole with a kitchen towel. Blend until smooth, stopping and scraping the sides blender with a rubber spatula if necessary. Let cool for a few hours before serving. This sauce will keep in an airtight container in the refrigerator for up to 2 weeks.

Jerk Sauce

YIELD: ABOUT 2½ CUPS

Use this classic Jamaican sauce to marinate any kind of meat before grilling, or use it straight from the container as a condiment.

5 GREEN ONIONS (WHITE AND LIGHT GREEN PARTS), CHOPPED

2 GARLIC CLOVES, SMASHED

2 SCOTCH BONNET OR HABANERO CHILES, STEMMED
    AND CHOPPED

½ CUP YELLOW ONION

¼ CUP DISTILLED WHITE VINEGAR

¼ CUP SOY SAUCE

1 TABLESPOON PACKED DARK BROWN SUGAR

1 TABLESPOON FRESH THYME LEAVES

1 TEASPOON WHOLE ALLSPICE BERRIES

1 TEASPOON GRATED GINGER

1 TEASPOON FINE SALT

½ TEASPOON BLACK PEPPER

¼ TEASPOON GROUND CINNAMON

2 TABLESPOONS VEGETABLE OIL

1 TEASPOON GRATED ORANGE ZEST

½ CUP FRESHLY SQUEEZED ORANGE JUICE

1. In a food processor fitted with a blade attachment, combine the green onion, garlic, chiles, yellow onion, vinegar, soy sauce, brown sugar, thyme, allspice, ginger, salt, pepper, and cinnamon. Process until smooth, stopping to scrape down the sides as needed.

2. In a large frying pan over medium heat, heat the oil. Add the mixture from the food processor and cook, stirring frequently, until fragrant, about 5 minutes. Remove from the heat and stir in the orange zest and orange juice. Let cool, transfer to an airtight container, and refrigerate for up to 2 weeks.

Note: If using as a marinade, make sure sauce is completely cooled before adding the meat, poultry, or seafood.

Hot Curried Caribbean Sauce

YIELD: ABOUT 2 CUPS

The prevalent curry flavor of this sweet, fruity sauce is a natural companion for poultry and pork.

10 SCOTCH BONNET OR HABANERO CHILES, STEMMED
    AND CHOPPED
1 CUP CHOPPED VERY RIPE MANGO
¾ CUP YELLOW MUSTARD
⅓ CUP DISTILLED WHITE VINEGAR
¼ CUP PACKED LIGHT BROWN SUGAR
1 TABLESPOON CURRY POWDER
1 TEASPOON GROUND CAYENNE PEPPER
1 TEASPOON GROUND CUMIN
¾ TEASPOON FINE SALT
½ TEASPOON FRESHLY GROUND PEPPER

In a blender, combine all of the ingredients and blend, stopping to scrape down the sides with a rubber spatula as necessary, until very smooth, about 1 minute. Transfer to an airtight container. The sauce will keep in the refrigerator for up to 1 week.

Sauce Chien

YIELD: ABOUT 2 CUPS

The literal French translation for chien *is "dog," but more likely, the less literal meaning of "having spunk" applies to this sauce. It gives boldness to simple grilled fish or vegetables.*

2 GARLIC CLOVES, CHOPPED

1 SCOTCH BONNET OR HABANERO CHILE, STEMMED AND CHOPPED

1 SHALLOT, CHOPPED

½ CUP EXTRA-VIRGIN OLIVE OIL

½ CUP ITALIAN PARSLEY LEAVES

¼ CUP FRESHLY SQUEEZED LIME JUICE

1 TABLESPOON CHOPPED FRESH CHIVES

2 TEASPOONS FINELY CHOPPED FRESH GINGER

1 TEASPOON FINE SALT

½ TEASPOON FRESHLY GROUND BLACK PEPPER

½ TEASPOON FRESH THYME LEAVES

In a blender, combine all of the ingredients and process, stopping to scrape down the sides of the blender with a rubber spatula as necessary, until very smooth. Transfer to an airtight container. The sauce will keep in the refrigerator up to 3 days.

Spicy Caribbean Sweet Potato Stew

YIELD: 6 SERVINGS

Coconut milk adds a silky texture to this healthy vegetarian stew. Drizzle more Ti Malice sauce over the top just before serving.

2 TABLESPOONS OLIVE OIL

2 CUPS CHOPPED YELLOW ONION

3 GARLIC CLOVES, FINELY CHOPPED

1 TABLESPOON FINELY CHOPPED FRESH GINGER

1 TEASPOON GROUND CORIANDER

1 TEASPOON FINE SALT

1 TEASPOON FRESH THYME LEAVES

1 TEASPOON GROUND TURMERIC

¼ TEASPOON GROUND ALLSPICE

4 CUPS VEGETABLE BROTH

3 CUPS SWEET POTATO, CUT INTO ½-INCH CUBES

3 CUPS CHOPPED KALE

ONE 15-OUNCE CAN DICED TOMATOES, DRAINED

ONE 15-OUNCE CAN BLACK-EYED PEAS, DRAINED AND RINSED

3 TABLESPOONS SAUCE TI MALICE (PAGE 90)

ONE 14-OUNCE CAN COCONUT MILK

2 TABLESPOONS FRESHLY SQUEEZED LIME JUICE

1. In a large pot or Dutch oven over medium heat, heat the oil. Add the onion and cook, stirring occasionally, until softened, about 10 minutes. Add the garlic, ginger, coriander, salt, thyme, turmeric, and allspice. Stir to combine, and cook until the spices are fragrant, about 3 minutes.

2. Add the vegetable broth and bring to a simmer. Add the sweet potato and kale and cook until the sweet potatoes are fork-tender, about 10 to 15 minutes. Stir in the tomatoes, black-eyed peas, and sauce Ti-Malice and return to a simmer. Stir in the coconut milk and lime juice, and heat until warmed through. Season with salt if necessary. Serve immediately with extra Sauce Ti Malice on the side.

Caribbean Black Beans and Plantains

YIELD: 4 SERVINGS

For this classic Caribbean dish, look for plantains that are dull yellow in color with patches of black, signaling their peak of ripeness. You'll want all of the natural sugars to caramelize during cooking. If you can't find plantains, firm, ripe bananas will work, too.

4 TABLESPOONS OLIVE OIL

1 CUP CHOPPED YELLOW ONION

3 GARLIC CLOVES, FINELY CHOPPED

2 TEASPOONS CHILI POWDER

1 TEASPOON FINE SALT

½ TEASPOON GROUND CUMIN

¼ TEASPOON GROUND CINNAMON

TWO 15-OUNCE CANS BLACK BEANS, DRAINED AND RINSED

¾ CUP WATER

2 TABLESPOONS CARIBBEAN-STYLE HOT SAUCE (PAGE 92)

2 RIPE PLANTAINS, PEELED

FRESHLY SQUEEZED LIME JUICE, FOR DRIZZLING

1. In a medium saucepan over medium heat, heat 2 tablespoons of the oil. Add the onion, garlic, chili powder, salt, cumin, and cinnamon. Cook, stirring occasionally, until the onions are soft and just beginning to brown, about 5 minutes.

2. Add one-third of the beans and mash completely with the back of a spoon or a potato masher. Add another third of the beans and mash completely, stirring occasionally. Add the remaining third of the beans

and mash, leaving about half of the beans intact. Continue cooking, stirring constantly, until the bean starches begin to coat the bottom of the pan and turn golden brown, about 3 minutes.

3. Add the water and hot sauce, and bring to a simmer. Cook, stirring and scraping the bottom of the pan to incorporate the water, until the beans are heated through, about 2 minutes. Remove from the heat. The beans will thicken as they cool.

4. Slice the plantains in half lengthwise; then cut the halves crosswise into 2-inch pieces. In a large nonstick frying pan over medium-high heat, heat the remaining 2 tablespoons of oil. Place the plantains cut-side down in the pan, season with salt, and cook until golden brown on the bottom, about 3 minutes. Transfer to a plate. Place a serving of the beans in a shallow bowl, top with the plantains, and drizzle with a little of the lime juice.

Spice-Rubbed Rack of Lamb

YIELD: 4 SERVINGS

Toasting the spices for this rub is a crucial step for maximum flavor. A spice grinder works best, but a mortar and pestle does the job just as well.

ONE 2- TO 2½-POUND FRENCHED 8-BONE RACK OF LAMB,
　　FAT CAP TRIMMED TO ¼ INCH
2 TABLESPOONS WHOLE ALLSPICE BERRIES
2 TABLESPOONS BLACK PEPPERCORNS
1 TABLESPOON PACKED LIGHT BROWN SUGAR
2 TEASPOONS CUMIN SEEDS
2 TEASPOONS FINE SALT
3 TABLESPOONS OLIVE OIL
JAMAICAN SCOTCH BONNET PEPPER SAUCE (PAGE 94)

1. Preheat the oven to 350°F and arrange a rack in the middle. Let the lamb sit at room temperature while the oven preheats.

2. In a spice grinder, combine the allspice, peppercorns, sugar, and cumin, and grind into a fine powder. Transfer to a small bowl and stir in the salt. Sprinkle the lamb all over with the spice rub and set aside.

3. In a large oven-safe frying pan over medium-high heat, heat the oil. Place the lamb fat-side down in the pan and sear, turning to sear all surfaces, until golden brown, about 4 minutes total. Turn the lamb fat-side up and transfer to the oven. Roast until an instant-read thermometer inserted into the center registers 125°F to 130°F for rare, about 25 to 35 minutes. Transfer the lamb to a cutting board and let rest uncovered for about 15 minutes before carving. Serve drizzled with the pepper sauce.

Jerk-Marinated Barbecue Chicken

YIELD: 6 SERVINGS

Thighs and drumsticks are the juiciest parts of the chicken, complementing the assertive jerk marinade well. You can use chicken breasts instead, but make sure to keep the bones and skin intact so they don't dry out during cooking.

3 POUNDS BONE-IN, SKIN-ON, CHICKEN THIGHS AND DRUMSTICKS
2 CUPS JERK SAUCE (PAGE 98), PLUS MORE FOR SERVING
VEGETABLE OIL FOR GRILLING

1. Preheat a grill. Place the chicken in a 9-by-13-inch baking dish. Pour 1½ cups of the Jerk Sauce over the chicken. With your hands, rub the sauce into the chicken, until evenly coated. (If not cooking chicken right away, cover and refrigerate for up to 24 hours.)

2. Rub the grill grates with a towel dipped in vegetable oil. Place the chicken on the grill, skin-side down. Cover the grill and cook until grill marks appear on the bottom of the chicken pieces, about 5 minutes. Flip over the chicken, cover the grill, and cook until grill marks appear on the second side, about 5 minutes more.

3. Flip the chicken again and brush a thin coating of the remaining Jerk Sauce over the chicken. Cover the grill and cook the chicken for 5 more minutes. Repeat this process every 5 minutes to slowly build a delicious layer of jerk flavor. Grill the chicken until an instant-read thermometer inserted into the thickest piece reads 160°F to 165°F and the meat near

continued ▶

Jerk-Marinated Barbecue Chicken *continued* ▶

the bone is no longer pink, about 10 to 15 minutes more (about
25 to 30 minutes total cooking time). Transfer the chicken to a clean
serving platter and serve with extra Jerk Sauce.

Note: If using chicken that has been marinating in the refrigerator, let it sit at room
temperature for about 15 minutes before grilling.

Pan-Seared Halibut with Sauce Chien

YIELD: 4 SERVINGS

Halibut is a thick and hearty fish that can stand up to the flavor of this intense sauce. If you don't want to sear it in a pan, grilling is a good alternative.

FOUR 4- TO 6-OUNCE, 1- TO 1½-INCH-THICK SKINLESS
    HALIBUT FILLETS
SALT
FRESHLY GROUND PEPPER
2 TABLESPOONS OLIVE OIL
SAUCE CHIEN (PAGE 101)

1. Pat both sides of the fish dry with paper towels and season both sides with salt and pepper.

2. In a large heavy-bottomed frying pan or cast-iron skillet, heat the oil over medium-high heat. Add the fish and cook until the edges begin to turn opaque and the fish releases from the pan, about 3 minutes. Using a flat metal spatula, flip over the fish and cook until firm to the touch and opaque in the middle, about 3 to 5 minutes more. Place the fish on plates and drizzle with Sauce Chien.

ASIA

Sriracha

YIELD: 1 CUP

Replicate the well-known commercial sauce by starting with a fermented base of chiles. For a fast and easy version, you can skip this step, but the sauce will have much less depth of flavor.

11 OUNCES RED JALAPEÑO CHILES

4 TEASPOONS FINE KOSHER SALT

⅓ CUP PURIFIED WATER

¼ CUP WHITE WINE VINEGAR

4 TEASPOONS PACKED DARK-BROWN SUGAR

3 GARLIC CLOVES, CHOPPED

1. Set three chiles aside. Spread out the remaining chiles on a baking sheet and put them in a sunny spot for 2 days, or until soft and wrinkled.

2. Stem the chiles, slice them lengthwise, and put them in a large bowl. Sprinkle with the salt. Using a potato masher, smash the chiles until only large chunks remain. Set aside at room temperature uncovered for 24 hours.

3. Transfer the chiles and any of the accumulated liquid to a 1-quart mason jar with a two-piece lid. Pour the water into the jar, loosely fit the lid on the jar, and place the jar on a plate. Let the mixture sit at room temperature until it begins to fizz over and the peppers shrink, about 1 to 2 days.

4. Place the remaining three whole chiles on top of the mixture to make sure the mashed chiles are submerged under the liquid. Loosely replace the lid and let sit at room temperature to ferment at least 1 week and up to 2 weeks. (You may need to add more purified water to the jar to keep the chiles submerged.)

5. Wearing food handler's gloves, remove the whole chiles from the jar and discard. Transfer the mashed chiles and the liquid to a large bowl. Remove the seeds, leaving them behind in the liquid. Transfer the seeded chiles to a blender. Place a mesh strainer over a large measuring cup and strain the seeds from the liquid. Discard the seeds. Add the liquid to the blender.

6. In a small saucepan over medium heat, combine the vinegar and the sugar, stirring until the sugar dissolves. Add to the blender along with the garlic. Blend until smooth, stopping and scraping the sides of the blender with a rubber spatula as needed. Strain through a mesh strainer and discard the solids. Transfer to an airtight container. The sriracha will keep in the refrigerator for up to 6 months.

Sambal Oelek

YIELD: ABOUT 1 CUP

This simple recipe is ideal for beginners in hot-sauce making. Stir a spoonful into noodle dishes or an Asian-inspired soup.

½ CUP RED JALAPEÑO CHILES, STEMMED AND CHOPPED
3 THAI CHILES, STEMMED AND CHOPPED
1 TEASPOON FINE SALT
½ TEASPOON GRANULATED SUGAR
4 TEASPOONS FRESHLY SQUEEZED LIME JUICE

Put all of the ingredients in a food processor fitted with the blade attachment and process until fairly smooth, stopping to scrape down the sides of the blender with a rubber spatula as needed. Transfer to an airtight container. The sauce will keep in the refrigerator for up to 1 week.

Spicy Peanut Sauce

YIELD: ABOUT 2 CUPS

*There are many versions of peanut sauce, some more spicy than others.
This recipe provides a base with which to begin. Add more lime, sugar,
fish sauce, or chiles to suit your taste.*

2 TEASPOONS TOASTED SESAME OIL

½ BUNCH FRESH CILANTRO, LONG STEMS REMOVED

⅔ CUP NATURAL PEANUT BUTTER (NO ADDED SUGAR)

¼ CUP PLUS 2 TABLESPOONS SOY SAUCE

ONE 3-INCH PIECE GINGER, PEELED AND CHOPPED

2 TABLESPOONS FISH SAUCE

2 TABLESPOONS FRESHLY SQUEEZED LIME JUICE

2 TABLESPOONS GRANULATED SUGAR

2 MEDIUM GARLIC CLOVES, PEELED AND SMASHED

1 JALAPEÑO, STEMMED AND CHOPPED

HOT WATER, AS NEEDED

Put all of the ingredients except the water in a blender. Blend until
smooth, stopping as necessary to scrape down the sides of the blender
with a rubber spatula. If the mixture is too thick, add hot tap water
1 teaspoon at a time until the desired consistency is reached. Use
immediately or transfer to an airtight container. This sauce will keep
in the refrigerator for up to 4 days.

Chinese Hot Chile Oil

YIELD: 1 CUP

Heating the oil to optimal temperature allows the chile flavor to infuse the mild, nutty-flavored oil. Peanut is the best choice for the oil in this recipe, but you can substitute vegetable oil instead. Stay away from olive oil, which should not be heated to high temperatures and has its own powerful flavor.

25 DRIED CHILES DE ÁRBOL, STEMMED AND FINELY CHOPPED
1 CUP PEANUT OIL

1. Put the chiles in a small heatproof bowl.

2. In a small saucepan over medium-high heat, heat the oil until it reaches 250°F on a deep-frying thermometer. Remove from the heat and let cool to 230°F. Pour the oil over the chiles. Cool completely.

3. Strain the oil into a 1-cup airtight container set over a fine-mesh strainer. This sauce will keep covered in the refrigerator for up to 1 month.

Korean Chile Sauce

YIELD: 1 CUP

This sweet sauce is the perfect accompaniment to Korean barbecue or even as a dipping sauce for crunchy fried egg rolls. You can find kochujang at a Korean market or online.

½ CUP KOCHUJANG (KOREAN CHILI PASTE)
¼ CUP HONEY
¼ CUP RICE VINEGAR

In a medium bowl, combine all the ingredients. Transfer to an airtight container. This sauce will keep in the refrigerator for up to 1 month.

Sweet Asian Chile Sauce

YIELD: ABOUT 2½ CUPS

There are many ingredients in this recipe, but once blended they create a harmonious and balanced sauce. Liberally drizzle it over grilled chicken and white rice.

1 CUP MAE PLOY SWEET CHILI SAUCE

½ CUP CHOPPED YELLOW ONION

⅓ CUP THAI BASIL LEAVES

⅓ CUP CILANTRO LEAVES

¼ CUP FRESHLY SQUEEZED LIME JUICE

3 TABLESPOONS SRIRACHA (PAGE 112)

2 TABLESPOONS TOASTED SESAME SEEDS

1 TABLESPOON KOCHUJANG (KOREAN CHILI PASTE)

1 TEASPOON FINE SALT

½ TEASPOON FRESHLY GROUND PEPPER

4 GARLIC CLOVES, PEELED AND SMASHED

4 GREEN ONIONS (WHITE AND LIGHT GREEN PARTS ONLY), CHOPPED

1 DRIED ANAHEIM CHILE, STEMMED AND CHOPPED

1 SERRANO CHILE, STEMMED AND CHOPPED

ONE 2-INCH PIECE FRESH GINGER, PEELED AND CHOPPED

In a blender, combine all of the ingredients and purée until smooth. Transfer to an airtight container. This sauce will keep in the refrigerator for up to 1 week.

Nuoc Cham

YIELD: ABOUT 1½ CUPS

The key to this sauce is the perfect balance of sweet, spicy, and sour ingredients. Play around with the proportions to create your own unique sauce.

¾ CUP WATER

¼ CUP FRESHLY SQUEEZED LIME JUICE

3 TABLESPOONS GRANULATED SUGAR

3 TABLESPOONS FISH SAUCE

2 THAI CHILES, CUT INTO PAPER-THIN SLICES

1 GARLIC CLOVE, FINELY CHOPPED

1. In a container with a tight-fitting lid, combine the water, lime juice, and sugar. Shake vigorously until the sugar dissolves.

2. Add the fish sauce, chiles, and garlic. Stir to combine. This sauce will keep in the refrigerator for up to 2 weeks.

Smooth Serrano-Cilantro-Mint Chutney

YIELD: 1 CUP

Mix this herbaceous sauce together with some yogurt for a spicy yet cool addition to a simple sandwich of Indian naan bread topped with cucumbers. This chutney is also great as a dipping sauce for crudités.

1 CUP PACKED CILANTRO LEAVES

1 CUP PACKED MINT LEAVES

1 SERRANO CHILE, STEMMED AND CHOPPED

¼ CUP CHOPPED RED ONION

2 TABLESPOONS FRESHLY SQUEEZED LEMON JUICE

½ TEASPOON FINE SALT

WATER AS NEEDED

In a blender, combine all of the ingredients and blend, scraping down the sides of the blender with a rubber spatula as needed. Add water 1 tablespoon at a time until the mixture becomes a smooth paste.

Biber Salcasi

YIELD: ABOUT 1½ CUPS

This classic pepper paste is commonly used in Turkish cuisine and is stirred into many dishes to add spiciness. Try mixing a dollop into hummus for an added kick.

1 POUND SWEET RED CHILES, STEMMED AND CHOPPED
1 RED JALAPEÑO CHILE, STEMMED AND CHOPPED
1 TEASPOON FINE SALT
EXTRA-VIRGIN OLIVE OIL, FOR COVERING THE PASTE

1. Put the chiles in a food processor fitted with the blade attachment and process until they form a smooth paste.

2. Transfer the paste to a medium frying pan over medium heat. Stir in the salt and bring to a simmer. Cook, stirring occasionally, until the raw flavor is cooked out, about 15 minutes. Remove from the heat and let cool.

3. Transfer to an airtight container and cover the paste by ¼ inch with olive oil, replacing the oil as you use the paste to extend the shelf life. Covered with olive oil, Biber Salcasi will keep in the refrigerator for up to 1 month.

Adzhika

YIELD: ABOUT 2 CUPS

Use this Georgian pepper paste as a marinade for lamb or beef. It's also commonly served with melon as a first course or appetizer; or instead of melon, try it with tomatoes.

6 GARLIC CLOVES, CHOPPED

4 RED JALAPEÑO CHILES, STEMMED AND CHOPPED

2 RED BELL PEPPERS, STEMMED AND CHOPPED

1 CUP CILANTRO LEAVES

1 CUP TOASTED WALNUTS, CHOPPED

⅓ CUP RED WINE VINEGAR

2 TEASPOONS GROUND CORIANDER

1 TEASPOON DRIED MARJORAM

1 TEASPOON DRIED MINT

1 TEASPOON FRESHLY GROUND PEPPER

1 TEASPOON DRIED SAGE

½ TEASPOON FINE SALT

In a food processor fitted with a blade attachment, combine all of the ingredients and pulse. Scrape down the sides of the processor with a rubber spatula and process until the paste reaches the desired consistency. Transfer to an airtight container. Adzhika will keep in the refrigerator for up to 1 week.

Red Rooster Cocktail

YIELD: 1 DRINK

Sriracha is a spicy addition to most any food, but mixing it into a savory cocktail is a new approach. This drink, similar to a Bloody Mary, tastes best while enjoying brunch on a beach (in Phuket).

ONE 12-OUNCE THAI LAGER, SUCH AS SINGHA, CHILLED

2 OUNCES TOMATO JUICE

1 OUNCE LIME JUICE

1 TEASPOON SRIRACHA (PAGE 112)

PINCH OF FRESHLY GROUND PEPPER

PINCH OF SALT

ICE

LIME WEDGE

1. Put a pint glass in the freezer to chill for 10 minutes.

2. Pour the beer into the glass. Combine the remaining ingredients in a cocktail shaker filled halfway with ice. Shake vigorously, strain over beer, stir gently to combine, and serve with the lime wedge.

Curried Cauliflower

YIELD: 4 SERVINGS

This healthy cauliflower recipe is packed with flavor from the dry spices. Topping it with chutney gives it a fresh punch of flavor.

2 TABLESPOONS VEGETABLE OIL

¼ TEASPOON FENNEL SEEDS

½ YELLOW ONION, FINELY CHOPPED

1 TABLESPOON PEELED AND GRATED GINGER

1 GARLIC CLOVE, FINELY CHOPPED

1 TEASPOON GARAM MASALA

¼ TEASPOON TURMERIC

¼ TEASPOON CAYENNE PEPPER

SALT

½ CUP PLUS 2 TABLESPOONS WATER

1½ POUNDS CAULIFLOWER, TRIMMED AND CUT INTO 1-INCH FLORETS

¼ CUP CHOPPED CILANTRO LEAVES

2 TABLESPOONS FRESHLY SQUEEZED LEMON JUICE

SMOOTH SERRANO-CILANTRO-MINT CHUTNEY (PAGE 120)

1. In a large skillet over medium heat, heat the oil. Add the fennel seeds and toast, stirring until fragrant, about 1 minute. Add the onion, ginger, and garlic and cook, stirring with a wooden spoon, until browned, about 5 minutes.

2. Add the garam masala, turmeric, cayenne, and a large pinch of salt. Stir while drizzling in 2 tablespoons of water. Add the cauliflower and the remaining ½ cup water. Cover and cook until the cauliflower is tender, about 15 to 20 minutes.

3. Stir in the cilantro and lemon juice, and serve immediately with the chutney.

Creamy Eggplant Dip

YIELD: 6 TO 8 SERVINGS

Eggplant has a reputation for being watery and bitter, but roasting it in the oven and blending it until smooth reveals its creamy texture and earthy flavor.

ONE 1½-POUND GLOBE EGGPLANT, CUT IN HALF LENGTHWISE
1 CUP THICK GREEK-STYLE YOGURT
2 TABLESPOONS FRESHLY SQUEEZED LEMON JUICE
1 TABLESPOON BIBER SALCASI (PAGE 125)
¾ TEASPOON FINE SALT
1 GARLIC CLOVE, FINELY CHOPPED
EXTRA-VIRGIN OLIVE OIL FOR DRIZZLING
TOASTED PITA BREAD WEDGES OR PITA CHIPS

1. Preheat the oven to 475°F and arrange a rack in the middle. Line a baking sheet with aluminum foil and place the eggplant halves cut-side up on the baking sheet. Roast until very soft and the skin is wrinkled, about 40 to 50 minutes.

2. Scoop out the eggplant flesh and place it in the bowl of a food processor fitted with a blade attachment. Add the yogurt, lemon juice, Biber Salcasi, salt, and garlic. Process until smooth, scraping down the sides of the processor as needed, about 30 seconds.

3. Transfer to a shallow serving dish and drizzle with the oil. Serve at room temperature or chilled, with pita wedges or chips.

Grilled Chicken Satay

YIELD: 8 TO 10 SERVINGS

Chicken marinated in a spicy mixture of coconut milk, fish sauce, and curry paste makes for a classic pairing with peanut sauce. Make sure to let the excess marinade drip off before grilling so that it doesn't burn on the chicken.

1 CUP UNSWEETENED COCONUT MILK

4 TEASPOONS FISH SAUCE

4 TEASPOONS PACKED LIGHT-BROWN SUGAR

2 TABLESPOONS RED CURRY PASTE

1 TEASPOON FINE SALT

2 POUNDS BONELESS, SKINLESS CHICKEN BREASTS AND THIGHS

THIRTY 8-INCH WOODEN SKEWERS SOAKED IN WATER
    FOR AT LEAST 30 MINUTES

VEGETABLE OIL FOR THE GRILL

SPICY PEANUT SAUCE (PAGE 115)

1. In a large bowl, whisk together the coconut milk, fish sauce, brown sugar, curry paste, and salt; set aside.

2. Cut the chicken lengthwise into ½-inch-thick pieces and place in the marinade. Stir to coat the chicken and refrigerate for at least 30 minutes or cover and refrigerate for up to 24 hours.

3. Heat a grill pan or grill to medium-high (about 375°F to 425°F). Meanwhile, thread a piece of chicken lengthwise onto each skewer and transfer to a baking sheet.

4. When the grill is ready, lightly brush the grates with vegetable oil. Place the skewers on the grill, close the cover (if using a grill pan, cover with foil), and cook until grill marks appear on the bottom, about 3 to 4 minutes. Flip over the chicken, close the grill, and cook until grill marks appear on the second side and the chicken is cooked through, about 3 to 4 minutes more. Transfer the skewers to a clean serving platter and serve with Spicy Peanut Sauce for dipping.

Beef Bulgogi (Korean Barbecued Beef)

YIELD: 4 TO 6 SERVINGS

This is a classic Korean dish. The key to good bulgogi is uniform thinly sliced beef, so take your time when cutting for the best results. If the beef is partially frozen, it is easier to slice.

4 MEDIUM GARLIC CLOVES, CRUSHED

4 GREEN ONIONS (WHITE AND LIGHT GREEN PARTS), CUT INTO
3-INCH PIECES

1 YELLOW ONION, HALVED AND THINLY SLICED

½ CUP KOCHUJANG (KOREAN CHILI PASTE)

¼ CUP TOASTED SESAME SEED OIL

¼ CUP SOY SAUCE

3 TABLESPOONS KOREAN RED PEPPER POWDER

3 TABLESPOONS TOASTED SESAME SEEDS

3 TABLESPOONS GRANULATED SUGAR

2 TABLESPOONS SAKE OR MIRIN

2 POUNDS PARTIALLY FROZEN FLANK STEAK

VEGETABLE OIL FOR THE GRILL

KOREAN CHILE SAUCE (PAGE 117)

1. Put the first ten ingredients in a large resealable bag or bowl and stir to combine; set aside.

2. Slice the beef against the grain and on the bias into ¼-inch-thick pieces that are about 1½ inches wide. Add to the marinade and refrigerate 1 hour, or cover and refrigerate overnight.

3. Heat a grill to high (about 425°F to 450°F) and brush the grates with vegetable oil. Remove the beef from the refrigerator and let sit at room temperature while the grill is heating, at least 20 minutes. Remove the beef from the marinade and let the excess drip off. Grill uncovered until crispy and lightly charred, about 10 to 15 minutes total. Serve with the Korean Chile Sauce for dipping.

CHAPTER EIGHT

BEYOND

Chile Pepper Water
(Chili Peppa Watah)

YIELD: 16 OUNCES

The name really does say it all—this water is laced with heat from the chiles. Mirin adds a little sweetness; if you can't find Hawaiian salt, use coarse sea salt instead.

16 OUNCES WATER

15 THAI CHILES, FINELY CHOPPED

2 GARLIC CLOVES, FINELY CHOPPED

1 TABLESPOON MIRIN

1 TEASPOON COARSE WHITE HAWAIIAN SALT

1. In a large saucepan over high heat, bring the water to a boil. Add the remaining ingredients. Reduce the heat to low and simmer for 15 minutes. Remove from the heat and let cool completely.

2. Using a funnel, transfer the chile pepper water to an airtight container, and store in the refrigerator for up to 6 months.

Brava Sauce

YIELD: ABOUT 1½ CUPS

This sauce is usually seen as a main component on patatas bravas, *which are a popular Spanish tapa of fried potatoes often accompanied with aioli. It tastes equally delicious on French fries.*

2 TABLESPOONS OLIVE OIL

¾ CUP FINELY CHOPPED YELLOW ONION

3 GARLIC CLOVES, FINELY CHOPPED

1 TEASPOON HOT PAPRIKA

½ TEASPOON RED PEPPER FLAKES

ONE 15-OUNCE CAN DICED TOMATOES

¼ CUP WATER

½ TEASPOON FINE SALT

1 BAY LEAF

PINCH GRANULATED SUGAR

2 TEASPOONS SHERRY VINEGAR

1 TEASPOON TABASCO-STYLE SAUCE (PAGE 70)

1. In a medium frying pan over medium heat, heat the oil. Add the onion and cook, stirring occasionally, until softened, about 8 minutes. Add the garlic, paprika, and red pepper flakes; stir to combine. Cook until fragrant, about 1 minute. Add the tomatoes and their liquid, water, salt, bay leaf, and sugar and bring to a simmer. Cook, stirring occasionally, until the sauce has thickened, is darker in color, and has reduced by about half, about 15 to 20 minutes. Remove the bay leaf and transfer the sauce to a blender.

continued ▶

Brava Sauce *continued* ▶

2. Remove the small cap in the blender lid, place the lid on the blender, and cover the hole with a kitchen towel. Blend until smooth, stopping and scraping the sides of the blender with a rubber spatula if necessary. Add the vinegar and Tabasco-Style Sauce and pulse to combine. Season with additional salt, vinegar, or Tabasco-Style Sauce as desired. Transfer to an airtight container. This sauce will keep in the refrigerator for up to 4 days.

Piri Piri Sauce
(Peri Peri, Pili Pili)

YIELD: 1½ CUPS

Brought to Africa by the Portuguese, this sauce is popular in both countries and is often seen paired with chicken.

10 RED THAI CHILES
4 GARLIC CLOVES, CHOPPED
½ CUP FRESHLY SQUEEZED LEMON JUICE
2 TABLESPOONS FINELY CHOPPED CILANTRO LEAVES
½ TEASPOON FINE SALT
¾ CUP OLIVE OIL

1. In a food processor fitted with the blade attachment, combine all of the ingredients except the oil. Process, stopping to scrape down the sides of the processor with a rubber spatula as needed, until finely chopped.

2. With the processor on low, slowly drizzle in the oil. Transfer to an airtight container, and store in the refrigerator for up to 1 month.

Harissa

YIELD: 1 CUP

This North African condiment nicely spices up lamb, but make sure to try it stirred into a vegetarian stew, chickpeas, or even slathered inside a pita with falafel.

4 OUNCES DRIED CHILES (SUCH GUAJILLO CHILES OR NEW MEXICO CHILES), STEMMED

½ TEASPOON CARAWAY SEEDS

½ TEASPOON CORIANDER SEEDS

½ TEASPOON CUMIN SEEDS

¾ TEASPOON FINE SALT

¼ CUP OLIVE OIL, PLUS MORE AS NEEDED

4 GARLIC CLOVES, CHOPPED

2 TABLESPOONS FRESHLY SQUEEZED LEMON JUICE

1. In a medium bowl, combine the chiles, cover with boiling water, and let sit until softened, about 20 minutes.

2. In a medium frying pan over medium heat, toast the caraway, coriander, and cumin seeds, until fragrant, about 4 minutes. Transfer to a spice grinder, add the salt, and grind to a fine powder. Set aside.

3. Drain the chiles and transfer to the bowl of a food processor fitted with the blade attachment. Add the ground spices, olive oil, garlic, and lemon juice and process, stopping as needed to scrape down the sides with a rubber spatula, until very smooth. Transfer to an airtight container and add enough additional oil to measure ½ inch above the paste. This sauce will keep in the refrigerator for up to 3 weeks.

Aji Criollo

YIELD: ABOUT 1 CUP

Use this Ecuadorian salsa verde *as a dipping sauce for flakey empanadas or to liven up a bowl of simple rice and beans.*

4 JALAPEÑO CHILES
3 GREEN ONIONS (WHITE AND LIGHT GREEN PARTS), CHOPPED
2 GARLIC CLOVES, CHOPPED
1 CUP CILANTRO LEAVES
¼ CUP OLIVE OIL
¼ CUP OF WATER
2 TABLESPOONS FRESHLY SQUEEZED LIME JUICE

In a food processor fitted with the blade attachment, combine all of the ingredients. Process, stopping to scrape down the sides as necessary, until finely chopped. Transfer to an airtight container. Store the salsa in the refrigerator for up to 3 days.

Roasted Beet Salad with Harissa Dressing

YIELD: 4 TO 6 SERVINGS

Earthy roasted beets mixed with creamy yogurt, harissa, and mint makes for a simple side dish to serve with grilled lamb kabobs.

¼ CUP GREEK YOGURT

¼ CUP PLUS 2 TABLESPOONS OLIVE OIL

2 TABLESPOONS FINELY CHOPPED FRESH MINT LEAVES

1 TABLESPOON HARISSA (PAGE 136)

1 TABLESPOON FRESHLY SQUEEZED LEMON JUICE

1 TABLESPOON FINELY CHOPPED SHALLOT

SALT

FRESHLY GROUND PEPPER

2 POUNDS BEETS, TRIMMED AND PEELED

1. In a large bowl, whisk together the yogurt, ¼ cup of the olive oil, mint, harissa, lemon juice, and shallot. Season with salt and pepper; set aside.

2. Preheat the oven to 375°F and arrange a rack in the middle. Cut the beets into 1-inch-thick wedges. Place wedges on top of a large piece of aluminum foil. Drizzle with the remaining 2 tablespoons of olive oil, and season with salt and pepper. Fold up the foil to completely enclose the beets and place in the oven. Roast until the beets are tender and easily pierced with a knife, about 45 minutes to 1 hour.

3. Carefully open the foil packet. In a large bowl, toss the beets in the dressing. Stir to evenly coat. Season with salt and pepper if necessary.

Crispy Baked Potato Wedges with Aji Criollo

YIELD: 8 SERVINGS

Crispy, spice-coated potatoes make the perfect vehicle for transporting a fresh and lively aji criollo green sauce.

4 RUSSET POTATOES, SCRUBBED

3 TABLESPOONS OLIVE OIL

1 TEASPOON FINE SALT

½ TEASPOON GROUND CORIANDER

½ TEASPOON GROUND CUMIN

½ TEASPOON FRESHLY GROUND PEPPER

AJI CRIOLLO (PAGE 137)

1. Preheat oven to 425°F and arrange a rack in the middle. Line a baking sheet with aluminum foil.

2. Cut each potato in half lengthwise into four wedges. Put the potato wedges in a large mixing bowl with the olive oil, salt, coriander, cumin, and pepper. Toss to evenly coat the potatoes.

3. Place the potato wedges, skin-side down, on the foil. Be sure to space evenly, so they cook uniformly. Bake for 40 minutes, or until well-browned, crusty, and fork tender. Serve immediately with Aji Criollo for dipping.

Spicy Ahi Tuna Poke

YIELD: ABOUT 2 CUPS

Make sure to use the freshest and best-quality fish for this recipe. Once prepared, serve the poke right away. To keep it extra-cold, set the serving dish over ice.

1 POUND SUSHI-GRADE AHI TUNA, CUT INTO ¾-INCH DICE

3 GREEN ONIONS (WHITE AND LIGHT GREEN PARTS),
    FINELY CHOPPED

3 TABLESPOONS FRESHLY SQUEEZED LIME JUICE

2 TABLESPOONS SOY SAUCE

1 TABLESPOON CHILE PEPPER WATER (PAGE 132

2 TEASPOONS TOASTED SESAME SEEDS

1 TEASPOON GRATED FRESH GINGER

1 TEASPOON TOASTED SESAME OIL

SALT

1. Put the fish in a cold serving dish.

2. In a large bowl, combine the remaining ingredients. Sprinkle the mixture over the fish. Serve immediately.

Broiled Cod with Brava Sauce

YIELD: 4 SERVINGS

Once this classic Spanish sauce is ready, the fish takes just minutes to broil. In Spain, this dish is typically prepared with hake fillets, but cod works well, too, as it is similar in taste and texture.

4 COD FILLETS (ABOUT 1½ POUNDS)
1 TABLESPOON OLIVE OIL
SALT
FRESHLY GROUND BLACK PEPPER
BRAVA SAUCE (PAGE 133)

1. Preheat the oven to broil and arrange a rack in the upper third.

2. Pat the cod dry with paper towels and coat with the oil. Season both sides with salt and pepper and place on a baking sheet. Broil until the fillets are opaque and cooked through, about 5 to 6 minutes. Serve with the sauce.

Braised Piri Piri Chicken Thighs

YIELD: 4 TO 6 SERVINGS

Chicken is a natural pairing with spicy piri piri sauce. Braising the thighs gives them tons of chile flavor. The savory hot sauce is great for spooning over rice.

3 POUNDS BONE-IN, SKIN-ON CHICKEN THIGHS

SALT

FRESHLY GROUND PEPPER

2 TABLESPOONS OLIVE OIL

1 CUP CHOPPED YELLOW ONION

2 TABLESPOONS FINELY CHOPPED FRESH GINGER

½ CUP PIRI PIRI SAUCE (PAGE 135)

½ CUP WHITE WINE

1 CUP LOW-SODIUM CHICKEN BROTH

2 TABLESPOONS PACKED LIGHT BROWN SUGAR

1. Preheat the oven to 375°F and arrange a rack in the middle.

2. Pat the chicken dry with paper towels; then season generously with salt and pepper. In a large, heavy-bottomed, ovenproof pot over medium-high heat, heat the oil. Place half of the chicken thighs in the pot, skin-side down, and cook until golden brown, about 5 minutes. Flip over and cook the other side until golden brown, about 4 minutes more. Transfer the thighs to a plate and repeat with the remaining chicken.

3. Reduce the heat to medium and add the onion and ginger and season with salt and pepper. Cook, stirring occasionally, until the onion softens, about 5 minutes. Add the Piri Piri Sauce and cook until fragrant, about 2 minutes. Pour in the wine, scraping the bottom of the pot to release any browned bits, and reduce the liquid by half, about 3 to 4 minutes.

4. Add the broth and brown sugar and stir to combine. Return the chicken pieces to the pot along with any accumulated juices. Turn the chicken to coat evenly, and bring to a boil. Confirm that the chicken is skin-side up. Place the pot in the oven and cook until the sauce is vigorously bubbling around the sides and the chicken, when cut with a knife, is no longer pink, about 40 minutes.

RECIPE INDEX

INDEX

Made in the USA
San Bernardino, CA
21 December 2019